VIRTUAL
SELLING

VIRTUAL SELLING

Going Beyond the
Automated Sales Force to Achieve
Total Sales Quality

THOMAS M. SIEBEL
MICHAEL S. MALONE

THE FREE PRESS
New York   London   Toronto   Sydney   Tokyo   Singapore

The Free Press
A Division of Simon & Schuster Inc.
1230 Avenue of the Americas
New York, N.Y. 10020

Printed in the United States of America

printing number

1 2 3 4 5 6 7 8 9 10

Text design by Carla Bolte

Library of Congress Cataloging-in-Publication Data
Siebel, Thomas M.
    Virtual selling : going beyond the automated sales force to
achieve total sales quality / Thomas M. Siebel, Michael S. Malone.
        p.   cm.
    Includes bibliographical references and index.
    ISBN 0-684-82287-3
    1. Sales management—Automation.   2. Information storage and
retrieval systems—Selling.   I. Malone, Michael S. (Michael Shawn),
1954–   .
HF5438.4.S5   1996   95–52004
658.8'1'00285—dc20   CIP

Contents

Chapter 1

Finding the Path

In slower times, achieving results was simpler. For leading organizations, outperforming competitors demanded little more than business as usual. Not so any more because intense competition is rendering historic success formulas obsolete. To continue achieving results in the future, organizations will need to compete in new ways, with new skills to satisfy ever-changing customer demands.

—*Andersen Consulting*
Outlook *1994*

In the last few years, companies have taken such warnings to heart.

They have been told they must flatten their organizations, re-engineer their processes, form "virtual" alliances with suppliers, distributors, and customers, and most of all, take advantage of the productivity leaps made possible by the rapid advances in information and communications technologies. The most successful firms in the United States, Japan, and Europe have done just that; one by one, their key operations—their "basic building blocks"—have been transformed.

Over the last two decades, accounting and finance, manufacturing, research and development, human resources, and customer support have all been transformed by technology. They have been automated, streamlined, been made more flexible, responsive, and adaptive. Ultimately, their success has resulted in reduced costs, increased productivity, and greater customer satisfaction.

We are now at the last great unautomated corporate frontier: sales.

The image is a resonant one. Sales is the untamed frontier of the business world: unpredictable, passionate, theatrical, full of eccentric characters, and dangerous to the newcomer. Like the frontier, the destiny of sales is to be explored, settled, and tamed by people using the right tools and technology. But many also will perish on this frontier, because they are unprepared, unnecessarily exposed to the elements, and annihilated by quick-footed and aggressive foes. The real question is: how many bones will lie bleaching in the desert or buried on Boot Hill before the new era finally arrives? And will you be one of those victims?

Sales force automation is rapidly rising to the forefront of the business computing market. According to *Personal Selling Power* magazine, " . . . whether managers realize it or not, automation has become an operating cost in the sales budget"—a cost which may rise as high as $12,000 per salesperson.[1] Right now, as this book goes to press, as many as 500 companies are rushing into the market offering information technology tools for sales.[2] Their target is the 9 million salespeople in the United States,[3] and perhaps four times more in the rest of the industrialized world. The sales automation software market was estimated to be $700 million in 1995 and is expected to reach as high as $10 billion by the turn of the century.[4] That makes it the fastest growing market segment in the computer software business.

Already, at least 2.5 million corporate salespeople have been affected in some way by automation or information sales tools.[5] In 1993, when *Computerworld* surveyed the information services departments of its largest corporate readers, 58 percent said that the user department receiving most of their attention was sales and marketing—compared to just 3 percent that named either research and development or corporate administration.[6]

Two of the largest system-integration companies in the world, Andersen Consulting and KPMG Peat Marwick, have now set up focused business practices deployed solely to deliver comprehensive turnkey Sales Force Automation solutions on a global basis to their large corporate customers. According to Phillip Tamminga, director of the Sales Effectiveness practice at Andersen Consulting, "We formed this practice in direct response to market forces. Quite simply, our largest customers are increasingly demanding a focused, highly specialized response to their growing sales automation requirements. We have rarely seen such dramatic growth in market demand."

Clearly we are seeing an extraordinary market shift. In the 1970s and early 1980s companies dabbled occasionally in this area to save on costs. By the end of the 1980s companies began to deploy early sales automation tools in an attempt to increase profitability and obtain strategic competitive advantage. Now the race to automate sales has taken on a life of its own. Companies are today treating the investment of millions of dollars on sales automation tools as if it is a matter of survival.

Why the rush to re-engineer sales?

• *Complexity:* It is getting more and more difficult to make a sale. One reason is that products themselves are getting more complicated. Thanks to programmability, manufacturing and design automation, and new delivery systems, many items that used to come in a couple of models and with a handful of options may now be available in thousands of permutations. In some cutting-edge industries, such as gate array circuits, even the traditional notion of "model" has disappeared, to be replaced by a set of capabilities. Clearly the days when a salesperson could carry the company catalog around in his or her head are rapidly disappearing. Instead, salespeople will now be designing products on the spot. But that can only happen if they are both trained to do that and supplied with constantly updated information on those capabilities.

That's only half of the challenge. Customers too are changing. With products becoming so complex, it is often the customers themselves who best know what they want . . . and more and more have a greater understanding of their supplier's offerings than their supplier's own sales force. Faced with such an "information affluent"[7] customer, a salesperson must have the relevant information at hand just to keep from impeding the sales process, much less drive it. Better yet, that salesperson needs the tools to *enlist* the customer in the product design and order process.

These two forces, product indeterminacy and customer sophistication, combine to create a radically new sales environment, one that is alien to traditional sales. As The Conference Board recently wrote:

> The salesperson is increasingly the "point person" who presents to the customer the combined efforts of separate company function: product development and design; advertising, merchandising and promotion; R&D and manufacturing, etc. In some instances, this is done by building customer relationships, acting as a consultant, and even co-producing the product with the customer . . . Contact is continuous, not only at the time of the sale, but before that, in design assistance and cooperation, and later, through service and follow-through.[8]

Needless to say, there are few sales departments today capable of such a balancing act.

• *Re-engineering:* One of the most obvious characteristics of the new corporation is the increasingly flat organizational structure. Many of the layers of middle management, whose historical role was to condense raw information flowing upward to top management and to elaborate on instructions flowing downward to line employees, have been stripped away. Replacing this hierarchy of managers are information networks, which automatically download new information to salespeople or present summaries to them the next time they log on to the automated information system. In practice such reorganization also means greatly expanded spans of control and increased responsibilities placed upon those managers who remain.

Sales, as one of the most traditionally-organized corporate operations, is a target ripe for restructuring. But therein lies a dilemma: every minute spent by a salesperson on administrative tasks once performed by others (word processing, filing, reporting) slices directly into the company's sales. Hence, the hurry to develop tools to simplify and speed up those ancillary tasks.

•*Global Competition:* In this age of increased international competition from nations with high levels of automation or low levels of employee pay, our need to cut costs is paramount. Agile corporations are lean corporations, with greater resources being shifted to product development (to remain ahead of the competition), manufacturing (to meet rapidly shifting demand), and customer service (to keep customers for the multiple generations it will now take to show a profit on product development). Inevitably, that means fewer resources for the other operations in the company. Internal pressures are at work as well: when resources are limited, and every department is tightening its belt, executive attention is focused on sales to become more efficient. Cost-cutting techniques using high technology are not only well-proven but also easily transferable from other operations. Not surprisingly, then, most early-generation sales automation tools have emphasized cost reduction.

•*Productivity:* Though rarely mentioned, productivity will provide the most important impetus for re-engineering sales. In fact, so overwhelming is the leverage that results from increasing the productivity of sales that most companies will embrace sales automation for this reason alone . . . or risk annihilation by their competitors. The reason for this is straightforward: sales is unique among corporate activities in that its productivity increases show up not only in terms of reduced costs but, more importantly, in *increased revenues*. The economic impact of increasing revenues, even while merely holding sales costs constant, is extraordinary.

For example, take a corporation with sales of $100 million per year and operating costs of $85 million, leaving a pretax profit of $15 million. If, through sales automation technology, it can increase its productivity by a modest 15 percent, its revenue is then increased to $115 million. While the expenses associated with sales typically decrease

SALES RE-ENGINEERING ECONOMICS
(in millions)

Revenues	$1.00	$1.15
Expenses		
COGS	0.30	0.33
Sales & Marketing	0.35	0.35
R&D	0.10	0.10
G&A	0.10	0.10
Total Expenses	0.85	0.85
Operating Margin	$0.15	0.30
Net Income	$0.08	$0.13

through automation as well, this example will assume that they are just held constant, or offset by an associated increase in cost of goods sold. Even then, with $115 million in revenue and $85 million in expenses, the pretax profit soars to 26 percent or $30 million, a *100 percent increase* in profitability.

There have been few times in the history of information technology where the mathematics of using it have been so compelling. The economic returns are immediate. They tend to be greater than those expected from any other information technology investment that the company has ever considered.

Think about it. When we automated finance, we were initially hoping for a 10 percent cost savings. When we first automated manufacturing, we were hoping for relatively small increases in production yields. When we implemented automation tools for general administrative office work, we were hoping to shave administrative personnel costs. The economic returns of these investments were calculated over three- to seven-year time periods just to reach the break-even point. In most cases, the improvements in profitability were almost imperceptible.

Never before in the history of information technology have the economics of the decision process been quite so clear as in sales. Moreover, this payback is immediate. The impact on the bottom line is easily measurable. The focus is not on cutting costs but on increasing productivity—directly affecting top line revenue production.

And a 10 percent productivity leap is conservative, say some observers of sales automation. According to Moriarty and Swartz in the *Harvard Business Review:*

Finding the Path

In cases we have reviewed, sales increases arising from advanced marketing and sales information technology have ranged from 10 percent to more than 30 percent, and investment returns have often exceeded 100 percent. These returns may sound like the proverbial free lunch, but they are real.[9]

As part of their research, Moriarty and Swartz looked at two companies that had invested in sales automation. One, a $7 billion electronics manufacturer, was a likely candidate to be receptive to the potential of high technology. But the other, an $8 billion custom printing company, was skeptical that technology could be harnessed to increase sales. Yet, Moriarty and Swartz found that *both* firms saw a first-year return on their sales automation investment of more than 100 percent.

The electronics concern installed a sales support system for more than 500 salespeople. Sales rose 33 percent, sales force productivity rose 31 percent and sales force attrition dropped 40 percent. The reduced attrition alone produced savings in recruiting and training costs that paid for the company's $2.5 million investment in less than 12 months. At the custom printer, an $80,000 investment in a minicomputer and telemarketing software returned a 25 percent increase in sales and attained payback in less than 6 months.[10]

That was in 1989, *before* the advent of affordable and powerful laptop computers, before electronic data interchange (EDI), distributed and replicated data bases, multimedia, wireless computing, video teleconferencing and practical client/server software architectures to drive mission-critical applications. These developments represent nothing less than a quantum leap in technologies that are immediately applicable to sales force automation and that will be harnessed to build solutions which create an equally dramatic impact on sales productivity. All of this suggests that increased revenue resulting from greater sales productivity— and thus increased profit—offers corporations their greatest leverage not only for remaining competitive, but to dominate their markets through explosive growth.

And yet . . .

Despite the power of the economic model, recent surveys have found that Sales Force Automation (SFA), as the technology is now called, can only be characterized as a failure within many of the firms which have attempted to implement it. A 1990 survey by The Conference Board found that half of all companies with operational sales automation systems reported "serious" shortcomings with their systems, and nearly half, if they could start over again, would choose a different vendor.[11]

In other words, most sales force automation tools *don't work*. Many, in fact, make the situation worse. The tantalizing prospect of spectacular productivity leaps remains just that for many companies.

Why? Because they get the model backwards. And worse, the sales automation industry has made a business out of reinforcing this error.

Organizations have historically oversimplified the process of selling, viewing it as based primarily on the ability of the sales representative to create and maintain strong personal relationships with prospects and customers. In practice, salespeople are typically given little more than leads and product literature and are expected to generate revenue. However, in reality selling is a complex and information-intensive process, often requiring the salesperson to act as an expert consultant and problem solver.

Most of the Sales Force Automation software that has been written and installed to date reflects this oversimplification of the sales process and uses automation as a means of cost reduction: word processors, spreadsheets, e-mail, contract managers, PIMs, and account and territory managers. The problem with such systems has been their focus on control of the sales force and analysis of sales-related information rather than on improving the effectiveness of the selling process. While some of these products have helped individual salespeople to increase their efficiency, they have done little or nothing to increase their ability to generate more revenue or shorten their sales cycle. Consequently, they have been received by salespeople with very little enthusiasm and have disappointed those in sales and executive managers who were expecting productivity miracles.

Only when a corporation's managers approach Sales Force Automation in an entirely different way, examining all the steps in the sales cycle and the key barriers to achieving sales, will they properly implement technology in sales, selecting and applying it only when it supports re-engineered sales processes.

This transformed demand will in turn force the creation of a new generation of Sales Force Automation applications designed to increase the effectiveness of the sales representative by providing opportunity management systems, marketing encyclopedias, product configurators, and "team selling" across multiple distribution channels. These systems will support the expanded role of the salesperson as sales project coordinator, linking all departments of the corporation and their information systems to satisfy the needs of the customer.

Using opportunity management systems, sales professionals will organize and track all information around the opportunity to convert a lead into a sale. Marketing encyclopedia systems will facilitate on-line access to all the product information, competitive information, sales literature, and sales tools, allowing a salesperson to create on-demand, customer-specific brochures and presentations.

Product configurators will give the sales representative the ability to assemble uniquely tailored products and services to meet the specific requirements of each customer. Sophisticated computer networks, data-base replication and synchronization, and collaborative groupware capabilities in sales force automation will allow enterprise-wide team selling. Intelligent messaging will link the sales representative with the rest of the organization, expediting approvals on discounts and proposals, confirming a visit from the president, and formalizing commitments from accounting and manufacturing.

With EDI technology, commitment requests will flow beyond the sales representative's own company, transmitting literature requests directly to fulfillment houses and confirming order and credit status directly to the customer. The information flow will be upward from the supporting company to the piloting sales professionals, empowering them to excel at their tasks.

Finding the Path

All of this is very exciting. Unfortunately, we appear to be heading in the opposite direction. As a result, even as these aforementioned technologies appear, they are put to the service of the wrong masters—and thus become meaningless, even destructive.

What is missing is a sense of perspective, an overall philosophy of sales that supports the salesperson, that resists the natural centripetal force of the home office, and that has an explicit, measurable goal beyond merely increasing sales contacts. That's why companies flirt with disaster if they merely attempt to bolt onto their existing sales organizations the latest and hottest SFA tool. Rather, they must begin by asking themselves the most basic question of all: *What does it mean to be a salesperson?* Those that do so honestly will find that they quickly come to place far less significance on *automating* the sales process and far more on *informing* the sales representative.

In particular, these companies find that to keep their sales force fully informed, they must:

- Equip salespeople with all of their leads, prospects, and contacts;
- Provide the facility to track, record, and communicate all of the history of an opportunity or an account;
- Support team selling and workgroup collaboration;
- Facilitate work flow and routing for approvals;
- Provide access to all relevant information on products, prices, competitors, and decision issues;
- Incorporate support for unique selling methodologies and processes that support sales cycle tracking and analysis;

- Provide salespeople with the ability to create custom presentations and on-demand, customized sales literature;
- Enable the salesperson to find the best combination of products and services based on a customer's unique profile;
- Empower that salesperson to make his or her own decisions, develop custom contracts and proposals and, acting as the customer's advocate, organize *ad hoc* interdepartmental company teams to serve as Virtual Selling™ organizations;
- Offer on-line sales training on sales process and new products and services;
- Automate the administrative tasks of recording, tracking, and reporting salespeople's appointments, activities, correspondence, literature fulfillment, expenses, and forecasts;
- Create closed-loop marketing and sales systems that assure complete traceability from marketing spending on lead generation through sales closure, product shipment, and customer support.

All of these actions share a common trait: *they place effectiveness above efficiency.* By using technology to serve the salesperson, organizations can dramatically increase the acceptance of technology by salespeople. Using technology to assist sales representatives in real *selling*—versus merely recording data—will dramatically affect their success and ultimately increase revenues, and that means larger commissions and a better career path within the organization. Early adopters of this technology who become informed sales representatives will soar ahead of their unautomated peers, enjoying more satisfied customers and consistently becoming top revenue producers. By comparison, sales representatives who do not attain expertise in using sophisticated technology in the selling process will become increasingly less and less marketable, and ultimately unemployable.

Call this new vision *Virtual Selling* to distinguish its flexible, sales process-oriented philosophy from the limited scope of today's administrative automation systems. Virtual Selling is the result of the application of the state of the art in management principles, information technology, and communications technology to the selling process. In the past three decades we have seen dramatic changes in management philosophies. The advances in the practical application of computer and communication technologies over this same period are simply mind-boggling. We offer you the road map for applying these advances to the sales process.

Applying Virtual Selling to the sales process we can achieve exceptionally high levels of sales effectiveness— because we now have exceptionally well-informed sales personnel. Informed salespeople can now fully appreciate their customers' needs. They can enjoy complete and accurate knowledge about their company's products and services—as well as those of their competitors. Now they can configure properly priced, yet highly customized, solutions to meet their customers' needs. They can become a sales force that learns, gaining an ever-richer understanding of its customers over time—thus providing constantly improving service and cementing ever-greater customer loyalty. We call this revolutionary body of sales personnel an *Informed Sales Force.*

What will a typical Informed Sales Force look like? For now, begin with a definition:

An Informed Sales Force uses technology to maximize the individual salesperson's selling time, provide complete access to all relevant corporate and market information to make the sale, and position that salesperson to independently make critical decisions that best serve both the immediate and long-term needs of the customer.

The implications of an Informed Sales Force are enormous, a revolution of the profession that will take decades to complete. But what is obvious right now is that the daily life of the salesperson of the future, the "informed" salesperson, will look very little like that life today. Some have suggested that these informed salespeople will more closely resemble modern product managers. But that is too timid. More accurately, they will resemble independent entrepreneurs directing their own businesses—developing long-term customer relationships, generating proposals, managing the configuration and creation of products and providing customer service and support . . . all the while linked by an electronic umbilical that is continuously sending massive quantities of information to and from a distant corporate headquarters.

But as powerful as an Informed Sales Force using Virtual Selling techniques would be, it is still incomplete without the combination of an operating philosophy and an empirical, measurable goal. This is the crucial step, because establishing such a goal acts as a regulator on innovation, assuring that as the Virtual Selling program grows and evolves it also stays on track, and that the Informed Sales Force doesn't exist only for its own sake, but for the ongoing success of the company.

This philosophy, derived from what has been learned over the last decade in manufacturing, is called *Total Sales Quality*™. It means precisely what it says: *perfection* in sales. Great leads, great pitches, irresistible closes and inevitable sales.

An Informed Sales Force using Virtual Selling to reach Total Sales Quality. It is an exhilarating vision. And it is possible. The time to start is now.

This book was written to explain that vision and how we get there. It is written not only for corporate management, but also for the millions of sales professionals—because, after all, if this vision is at all accurate they too will be chief executives of their own sales enterprises. From this day on, every salesperson should be the founder of his or her own sales start-up. Total Sales Quality, like most revolutions, will begin from the bottom.

The best way to understand the Total Sales Quality/ Informed Sales Force model is to see it in action. Not every company has swallowed the lure offered by SFA. Some have taken a different path. Though none have yet created a fully Informed Sales Force, some of the world's best companies are on their way.

One of these is Hewlett-Packard Co. of Palo Alto, California, one of the nation's oldest and most respected high technology firms. The company's story offers a vision of what can be accomplished through an intelligent, not knee-jerk, application of technology to sales.

Hewlett-Packard, founded in 1939 in a now-legendary

garage, is a worldwide electronics giant, with annual sales of $20 billion and 80,000 employees in 110 countries. At the heart of HP's success is a much-imitated business philosophy it calls "The HP Way," built upon the twin foundations of technical excellence and superior customer support.

Nowhere has this been more effectively done than in field sales. HP salespeople were expected to be as technically knowledgeable as electronics engineers (which many of them were), but also sufficiently empathetic and responsive to customers' needs to keep them loyal for generations. As numerous surveys over the years proved, HP's sales force did just that.

But by the late 1980s and the company's fiftieth anniversary, cracks were beginning to show in the HP Way. The company had grown so large, with so many employees scattered around the world, that some questioned if Hewlett-Packard could still be a "family." Field salespeople found themselves dealing with an increasingly monolithic home office that every year seemed less responsive. The company found itself for the first time losing sales in key businesses—computers, test and measurement instruments, and medical devices—to smaller and faster-moving competitors.

Said Dick Love, vice president of manufacturing for HP's Computer Systems organization, "The pace of change is so rapid that the ability to change has now become a competitive advantage."

A restructuring of the entire corporation was in order. Fortunately HP, unlike many other large U.S. technology firms, identified the need for change early. Even the founders, William Hewlett and David Packard, returned to the daily operation of the company to assist with the reorganization. Company operating divisions were restructured, new customer service systems were put into place, supplier lists were pruned and the relationships redefined for greater efficiency. As *Forbes* magazine would later write, HP "did what had to be done."

One of the biggest targets for re-engineering was sales. Not only had the historically warm relations between field sales and the home office become increasingly strained, but the salespeople were finding themselves increasingly buried under mountains of unmanageable information. Like many high-technology companies, HP had raced to bring more and more new products to market, until by the mid-1980s the rate of new product introductions approached one per work day. With dozens of possible permutations for each model, Hewlett-Packard salespeople found themselves representing a catalog with *6,000* different products.

Not surprisingly, product managers were complaining that their specific lines weren't getting enough attention from the field, while salespeople struggled to pick potential best-sellers out of the overall noise. Something clearly had to be done if sales performance was going to keep up with the changes going on in the rest of HP.

Being a company that sold others on the power of computers and communications gave Hewlett-Packard a head start. And, according to Dick Knudtsen, sales force productivity manager for the company's U.S. field operations, "We knew that our window of opportunity was narrowing." Accordingly, HP set out to rethink the entire sales operation of the company, searching for ways to use technology to improve performance.

The first area identified, in 1988, was speeding up the qualification of leads. HP instituted its Qualified Lead Tracking System (QUILTS). As Moriarty and Swartz describe it:

[QUILTS] electronically transmits inquiries to a telemarketing center, which qualifies and ranks them and electronically returns them to HP headquarters. The company has trimmed the turnaround time for leads from as much as 14 weeks to as little as 48 hours. Hot leads are handled even faster; they are telephoned to the field sales force from the telemarketing center.[12]

That was just the start. As a leader in client/server computer networks, Hewlett-Packard set about putting such networks to work inside the company. Where before, HP's customer response program had typically been handled by systems engineers on a rotating basis—resulting in varied-quality support—the company now set up a sophisticated computer-based Response Center with a permanent staff armed with database tools for tracking products and orders, searching for the solutions to common problems based upon keywords, sending software modifications to customers, and submitting modification requests to various engineering divisions. This not only enhanced the sales force's image with its customers, but removed from it what had been an added burden of acting as the customer's advocate to the company.

More remarkable, HP also set out to use technology to

help the salesperson before the sale. It organized a Professional Services Organization to provide potential customers with technical consulting, project management, training, and product transition planning. By 1993, HP had also created Electronic Centers of Expertise, regional demonstration centers which prospective customers could tour and where they could see simulated corporate environments with HP-based solutions at work.

The biggest challenge of all was that of keeping the sales force informed of what the company was doing. The first step was to abandon fifty years of geographic deployment and reorganize the force by industry focus. Recalls Wim Roelandts, senior vice president and general manager of HP's Computer Systems Organization:

> The tendency was to focus on a particular functional area which crossed industries, as an example R&D, or to develop an industry focus based on interest or opportunity. With the change to an industry alignment, we've minimized geographic obstacles by creating a sales business unit which focuses on customers in the electronics industry. This has enabled our salespeople to become far more knowledgeable with regard to the business issues electronics companies are facing and the application of information technology across the entire enterprise. Of course, we've taken advantage of our own experience as an electronics manufacturer in providing the sales force with the training and business insights required to add value to the customer.[13]

Sales training itself was revised to take advantage of technology. Before, HP had conducted nearly all of its new product training by bringing the entire 1,000-person sales force to a handful of classrooms—a process that consumed an average of three work weeks per salesperson per year, and cost $5 million for each two-day seminar. Now HP turned instead to video instruction and conferencing. Using the Hewlett-Packard Interactive Network (HPIN) developed by Tom Wilkins, the company's media technologies manager, salespeople could stay in the field and work while they learned. Yet instruction was not compromised because the salespeople could interact in real time with the instructors by voice transmissions or their networked HP 100 LX pocket computers.[14]

With HPIN, Hewlett-Packard salespeople can now be brought up to date on the latest products without leaving the sales office and with minimal reduction of the time they can spend selling—and at $80,000 per seminar with HPIN, Hewlett-Packard has seen a 98 percent reduction in training costs. Wilkins is now looking at ways to make the learning process even more flexible for the individual salesperson. "The network will move more toward an on-demand, just-in-time system as we add video servers so that programs can be stored and retrieved at each user's convenience," he says.[15]

The emphasis has now shifted to the individual salesperson. From the beginning of HP's restructuring of sales, the goal had always been to free the salesperson to *sell*.

According to Jim Kucharczyk, HP's national manager of sales programs for computer products, the company's efforts quickly focused upon where company salespeople were wasting productive selling time. It turned out to be the sales office itself. "When we looked at why they went to the office," he told *Performance* magazine, "we were surprised to learn that the biggest reason was to process the volumes of paper we were providing to equip them to sell the products. When our monthly newsletter hit eight-and-a-half pounds, we realized we had created the world's most highly paid filing clerks."[16]

By 1992, Knudtsen, Kucharczyk and others were leading the drive to keep the salesperson out in the field: the "virtual sales office," as it was called, supported by laptop computers, fax-modems, and pagers. Salespeople were now offered the choice of an office at home, an HP office without administrative support, or a rented efficiency office.[17]

But that mobilization of the sales force presented a host of new challenges, most notably in terms of motivation and the maintenance of team spirit. To that end, Knudtsen implemented programs to regularly and automatically share company news and information with all of the sales force. More importantly, he set about redefining the role of sales management to include maintaining morale and employee cohesiveness through regular communications and gatherings.

Says Knudtsen, "We don't want salespeople spending time in the office, but they get a lot from sharing ideas with other sales reps in social situations. So we ask the managers to make these opportunities available."[18]

Thanks to all of these changes at HP the very role of sales had begun to change. By the end of 1993, Roelandts would describe the company's sales force not as a revenue-generating operation, but as "a consultative partner." Something profound had happened. Now representatives from the sales force were being invited to contribute to product development and were asked to provide input to company direct marketing programs. Telephone salespeople now found themselves not only preceded by direct mail campaigns, but briefed by a massive database on each customer's purchasing history even before they made the call. The leads that resulted were now classified by the customer's likelihood of upgrading and instantly sent to the proper salesperson.[19]

As Hewlett-Packard approached its sixtieth anniversary, it had found new life. By rethinking its organization, and in particular, by applying technology to its sales operation, Hewlett-Packard had not only regained control over impending information overload, but increased its revenues and profits, and reduced its operating costs. While the other giants of the U.S. electronics industry found themselves in desperate straits by the early 1990s, HP restored itself to leadership.

From the trajectory of companies like HP we can trace forward to see a model for sales far different from anything proposed by Sales Force Automation—a model that is much more adaptive, organic, and most of all, not in command but commanded by the very human process of human beings selling to other human beings. What these companies are creating is an Informed Sales Force, and whether they have elaborated it or not, their goal is Total Sales Quality.

The rest of this book will be devoted to elaborating upon that model, showing why the Informed Sales Force is inevitable, how it works, and the best ways to evolve toward this model.

Finding the Path

Chapter 2 presents a vision of Total Sales Quality, and shows its antecedents in total quality programs in other parts of the corporation.

Chapter 3 sets the stage by looking at how sales are currently made, how those models and techniques date back a century or more, and why they are unlikely to survive.

Chapter 4 explains how the dynamo of technological innovation is forcing change; in particular, how developments in multimedia, telecommunications and the mobile office are forcing radical changes in both sales and marketing.

Chapter 5 shows how these old models are fading in the face of an explosion of hardware and software tools uniquely suited to sales.

Chapter 6 looks at how technology also will transform marketing, forcing the use of new tools, revamping the professions of marketing communications and, most importantly, reversing the old hierarchy of marketing "over" sales.

Chapters 7 and 9 then take an in-depth look at each of the areas where technology is having its most profound effect upon sales, including accessing information, reaching the customer, making the pitch, and configuring the right product.

Chapter 8 shows the Virtual Selling model at work, in clear contrast to traditional selling.

Chapter 10 presents a vision of life in an Informed Sales Force and suggests realistic, practical pathways for companies, large and small, to get there.

Total Sales Quality *is* the future of sales. Its intrinsic advantages make it inevitable. The real question is: which companies will recognize that fact and get there first? Which sales forces will see the need and force their companies to share their new philosophy? And which corporations will fail—through ignorance, inertia, or arrogance—to recognize the revolution erupting around them . . . and suddenly find themselves on the brink of extinction?

Chapter 2

Total Sales Quality

The TQM Movement hasn't reached sales yet, and that's where we need to go.

—Paul Selden, President

Sales Automation Association

Why is Sales Force Automation a failure? Why are so many firms disappointed with the early returns on their expensive investments in SFA?

The easy answer is ignorance. For many companies, automating the sales force simply means issuing the salespeople portable computers loaded with e-mail, spreadsheets, word processors and contact management programs—but no instructions on how to use any of this hardware and software—then expecting to see major productivity gains overnight.

A more sophisticated answer is misperception. Most of the Sales Force Automation programs currently on the market do nothing to help salespeople make *sales*. Rather, they are designed to help the salesperson wade through the ever-deeper swamp of administrative tasks—memos, reports, contracts, order forms, etc.—that characterize the modern corporation. Many companies are disappointed with the new tools because they expect them to help salespeople sell better—but, at best, these programs can only free up a little of the time salespeople spend (waste) on the corporate bureaucracy. Thus, salespeople may become more efficient with SFA, but rarely better.

These first two problems can be easily solved with a little training of employees and a lot more honesty from vendors. But there is a deeper, more disquieting, philosophical problem that lies behind these issues. And it is here that even the best-prepared and most careful company may founder. It is this flaw that underlies all of SFA, that may yet wreck the credibility of that industry . . . and take a number of customers down with it.

A vital clue can be found within the nomenclature itself. To have chosen a term like "automation," with all of its dark connotations of worker alienation and the primacy of systems over people, is more than a little suggestive about the mind-set of the industry's pioneers. And to look at most SFA programs is to see this philosophy made manifest.

Sales Force *Automation* implies that our sole task is to use technology to speed up previously inefficient operations. And, in fact, most current SFA systems misdirect salespeople away from selling and instead consume their time in creating reports and forecasts for management. That is to say, they aggravate precisely the disease they were supposed to cure.

Total Sales Quality

That's why many sales representatives understandably resist sales automation systems. The reason is obvious: living not in theory, but in the pragmatic reality of having to find leads and close sales, salespeople catch on quickly that these "tools" do nothing to help them become more successful in their jobs. And their reasonable response typically provokes an unreasonable reaction: management fiat that they use the new equipment or else. At its worst, this leads to a vicious cycle, in which sales devotes more and more of its precious time figuring out how to circumvent edicts from headquarters, while senior management invests in more and more automation hardware and software in the belief that the next purchase will finally make the difference and show positive results on the bottom line.

As *Business Week* wrote in 1993:

> . . . many self-motivated reps . . . perceived a "leash" around their necks, not a tool that would help them make more money. Many millions were wasted on wrongheaded, superficial automation schemes.[1]

This is the trap in which even the most enlightened and progressive corporate managements are finding themselves. And it is all done with the best intentions.

It is this underlying philosophical mistake that ultimately may undermine what is still a valid and important concept: using technology to improve the sales process. But if the problem is fundamental, then any solution also demands a rethinking of first principles. And that begins with understanding how the sales process really works, and how the people involved with it really behave.

That understanding will come from analyzing *all* of the steps involved in completing a sale, determining practical ways to streamline that process, establishing realistic metrics to measure performance—and only then creating information systems that facilitate and support the work process. Simplifying the bureaucratic process is important, but even more important is finding ways to help salespeople increase their sales by improving and increasing their focus on customers, expanding their services, and shortening the cycle to the close. Sales efficiency is good, but sales effectiveness is what we really need.

How do we get it? By reversing our emphasis from technology to people by investing in *sales information*, not sales automation. Our objective must not be to do more of what we have done in the past; not to make our goal that of more leads, more calls, more brochures, more proposals. Rather, our objective must be to help sales professionals to effectively understand and fulfill their customers' desires.

Even SFA advocates understand this. "It's vital to first understand what problems your salespeople are having," says Paul Selden, president of the Sales Automation Association. "If you give people the things they've been asking for all along—rather than blindly giving them laptops and some software—then they will buy into the automation system, and they'll *want* to use it."[2]

Ironically, by shifting our focus to people, we ultimately find ourselves directed back to technology. But this time, we know what we need: a comprehensive information system that provides—at the click of a mouse or the tap of a pen—everything that the sales professional or the customer might need to know: customer history, product options, competitive comparisons, recent articles, up-to-the-minute pricing, accurate order processing.

Where do we find this new sales philosophy? We already have it. We are just using it somewhere else. Our new guiding principle in sales is *quality.*

MANUFACTURING BEFORE QUALITY

For a century, from Eli Whitney through Frederick Taylor to River Rouge, manufacturing was a numbers game.

Production yielded a rather low ratio of good products to bad ones. Defects were seen as inevitable, and we responded to them by simply producing sufficient quantities to overcome the defect rate. For example, a company with a manufacturing defect rate of 50 percent would simply produce 2,000 units to fill a production goal of 1,000 units, discarding one out of every two items that came off the end of the production line.

Given that premise—that it was acceptable to manufacture bad products as long as you didn't ship them—manufacturing management as late as the 1970s was still primarily focused on increasing total production capacity. At every stage of the production process, defect rates were measured, and production and purchasing were adjusted accordingly. Quality control consisted of separating the bad finished products from the good ones. The "good" ones were shipped to customers. The "bad" ones ended up in the dumpster or sold at discount. Managers may have despaired over the waste and the lost revenues, but they saw no other choice.

Enter the computer, with its compelling ability to play this numbers game at the speed of light.

The first significant application of information technology to the manufacturing process was called *Computer Integrated Manufacturing* (CIM). CIM, introduced in the early 1970s, promised a dramatic increase in manufacturing capacity at each stage of the production process, creating more parts, more assemblies, more product on the shipping dock.

But missing from the CIM model, in fact not even included in its view of the production process, was the question of defect rates. CIM was simply the old production model, supercharged. So along with the dramatic increase in capacity came piles and piles of defective parts, defective assemblies, defective finished products literally scattered about factory floors and shipping docks. Sometimes, when demand outstripped supply, defective products were even shipped to customers to buy time for a later shipment of good products.

CIM's most famous victim was General Motors, which sank tens of billions of dollars into robots and computers that, as at the company's Hamtramck plant, damaged cars, hurt employees, and increased labor tensions. Similar disasters hit other companies in their rush to automate—until the phrase "Computer Integrated Manufacturing (CIM)" went from a catchword for progressive management to a sobriquet for a lemming-like pursuit of technology. Now desperate to salvage some of their investments, manufacturers revisited places like the Fremont, California,

NUMMI plant, where workers without robots were out-performing their counterparts in both the U.S. and Japan. Slowly they realized that what mattered was not the technology in itself but how it was applied towards a proper goal. In time, this new perspective came together in success stories like the Boeing 777, the Dodge Viper, and Motorola pagers.

In retrospect, CIM may well have been the single most visible failure in the history of the computer industry. Promised the moon, companies that blindly adopted CIM instead lost market share, money, and customers.

RADICALS TO THE RESCUE

It was against this backdrop of crisis that a radical new notion began to capture the attention of manufacturing managers everywhere. It was called *Total Quality* and was the brainchild of people like W. Edwards Deming and Philip B. Crosby.

Total Quality turned the traditional model of manufacturing on its ear. It was time, these thinkers argued, not only to stop accepting defects but to make working for their total elimination the new *raison d'être* of manufacturing. Manufacturing's new charter was to struggle for zero defects at every stage of the production process. And to do that, in turn, required companies to fundamentally alter the way they thought about manufacturing, the way they trained their people, and the way they managed.

So completely have we assimilated the notion of Total Quality Manufacturing that it is hard to remember what a radical notion this was in 1979 when Crosby published *Quality is Free* and a year later when Deming appeared in the television documentary "If Japan Can . . . Why Can't We?"[3]

Now, under TQM, instead of sweeping defective parts onto refuse piles, we would critically examine each one. We would understand how the defect was generated, and we would make certain that the same defect did not occur again. Each individual defect was now to be considered a systems failure. And from our suppliers, we would no longer accept "reasonable" defect rates—now we would demand 100 percent conformance to specifications.

Henceforth, quality would be described as conformance to our customers' requirements, rather than design specs— once again a reversal of perspective. And, by the same token, quality control would include the measurement of processes, rather than simply the inspection of finished products.

Total Quality Manufacturing changed manufacturing forever. It wasn't just a fad, because it was hard to argue with TQM's results. The companies that adopted the model quickly realized dramatic increases in productivity, employee job satisfaction, product quality, and profitability. Customer satisfaction rose, and market share grew. Widely adopted in Japan, TQM helped Japanese industry attain global domination in the automotive and consumer electronics industries. Total Quality Manufacturing became Japan's less-than-secret weapon.

U.S. companies, ignoring their homegrown theorists, soon found themselves faced with either signing on or risking annihilation. They made the right choice. In 1979, as

Total Sales Quality

Ford Motor Company lost $1.6 billion, company chairman Philip Caldwell announced that from now on quality came first. Ford embarked on a TQM program that included visiting Japan, hiring Dr. Deming, and committing the company to TQM under the rubric "Quality is Job One." By 1983, the company was already seeing dramatic improvements. Warranty repair frequencies dropped by 45 percent, and the number of "things gone wrong" reported by new car owners fell by more than 50 percent. In the same period, Ford's share of the U.S. car market rose to 19.2 percent, the highest it had been in five years. By 1984, total sales of cars, trucks, and tractors were 5.7 million, up 700,000 over 1983. There were record profits of $4.3 billion before taxes and operating costs had been reduced by more than $4.5 billion. Ford was now spending $12 million *less* a day than it had been five years before.[4]

Ford wasn't the only U.S. company to appreciate the value of TQM:

> . . . beginning in 1984, the Campbell Soup Company revised its recipe. With 44,000 employees and close to $4 billion in 1984 sales, the giant food corporation embarked on an internal Total Quality Management plan inspired by Deming's philosophy and modeled after many Japanese companies' implementations. They focused on "intrapreneurism," harnessing independent entrepreneurial attitudes of all their employees, statistical process control in their manufacturing, and vendor partnerships. Focused on well-trained and empowered workers and smoothly and efficiently running systems, Campbell has dramatically improved quality and increased productivity.[5]

Today, TQM is the *de facto* operating doctrine of almost every U.S. manufacturer. In the modern economy, either you play the TQM card or you don't play at all.

YESTERDAY'S SALES FORCE

Looking at Sales Force Automation and hearing the claims being made for it, one cannot help but see sobering parallels to the disaster of CIM. Today's salespeople live in the world of yesterday's manufacturing plant. For them, technology, misapplied, is at best an obstacle and at worst a threat. Quality is an alien concept. And if these congruences are real, then as we commit ourselves to SFA, we may be heading towards a debacle even bigger than CIM, because the effect will be amplified on the bottom line.

Is there such a parallel between sales and manufacturing? Yes. Sales, like manufacturing, is a process consisting of a number of stages: lead generation, lead qualification, sales presentation, proposal generation, and finally, the close.

To manage this process sales theorists have developed the concept of the "sales funnel." The sales funnel is a visual and conceptual representation of the various hurdles a lead must cross to become increasingly more qualified and eventually close. The top of the funnel is generally represented as a wide hopper, containing many leads. In *Strategic Selling*, Miller Heiman defines a lead in the top of the funnel as one whose data "suggests" there is a fit between a vendor's product or service and the prospective buying company's needs. A qualification process takes place at every stage in the sales cycle. Many leads are rejected, and only those whose data "verifies" that there is a possible order in the future remain in the funnel, becoming further qualified as bona fide opportunities. As each opportunity moves sequentially through the various stages of the sales cycle, the expected time to the order and the level of uncertainty involved are reduced—until only the best flow into the narrow neck of the funnel that represents the close.

A company's average sales cycle can be tallied as the amount of time it typically takes to move an order from the top to the bottom of the sales funnel—that is, the amount of time between the initial contact and the agreement to buy. And the lead-to-close ratio can be calculated by comparing the percentage of leads that ultimately close compared to the total number of leads initially generated.[6]

These sales tools, the sales funnel and the sales cycle, implicitly recognize very high "defect" rates at each stage of the process. In fact, they exist to navigate around these defects. The primary focus of sales management becomes the management of the sales funnel; in particular, it assures that the level of activity at each stage is sufficient to meet the revenue objectives of the organization. Thus, sales management is about playing the numbers: If we have 100 leads, we are safe. . . . If we generate ten bona fide sales proposals, history tells us we should meet our revenue number.

Needless to say, these numbers vary from industry to industry, and company to company, as does the time required to complete each stage of the process. Some companies and some industries have defect rates of only 90 percent, but others can be as high as 99.75 percent (that is, 99.75 percent of leads never amount to anything—see Chapter 3). And the 99 leads that were not suitable? The nine proposals that were not accepted? The two forecasted opportunities that were lost to competitors? What do we do about them? Just like the old factory, we sweep them up like faulty parts and discard them. And then we set about generating 100 new leads.

CIM IN SALES—A LESSON UNLEARNED?

What then does SFA bring to this archaic sales process? More of the same. More and more leads. More presentations. More proposals. More. More. More. And ultimately more and more prospective customers who have chosen *not* to do business with us. More inappropriate leads. More misfocused sales presentations. More unaccepted proposals. It is CIM brought to the sales office . . . and, as with CIM, the result is a deeper pile of defective parts on the factory floor.

We have been down this path before. We are recapitulating the past rather than learning from it. This time, however, the stakes are even bigger. As with CIM, no matter what is said in the brochures and advertisements, to date most of the application of computer technology to the selling process is not for the benefit of salespeople, but for sales management. It is about *control*, not empowerment. And the flow of information is upward, not downward.

Managerial control is the hidden agenda that salespeople intuitively understand, and resist. The secret objective is to get information from the field, not to provide it. The salesperson is expected to enter information, not to use it. SFA claims to be about enhancing a salesperson's productivity, but just as often it is really about monitoring that individual's performance.

As with CIM, with its dehumanization and replacement of workers, most contemporary SFA systems are fundamentally contemptuous of the sales professionals, believing that their human weaknesses—laziness, disorganization, incompetence—can be overcome with microprocessors and disk drives. And, again like CIM, the only real benefits accrue to management, not to the salesperson. And, ultimately, not to the customer.

Not surprisingly, just as CIM assembly lines produced worker revolt and even subversion, so too is sales force automation beginning to create its own neo-Luddites, and environments where each "improvement" results in more resistance than gains, with diminishing returns rather than productivity breakthroughs.

This is hardly the way to get to the informed sales force of the future. Without exception, systems of this type inevitably break down. Some of these failures have been very large and very expensive—often cause a very noisy and expensive crash.

If history provides a warning, it also offers a solution. When CIM went off the tracks, companies were desperate for an alternate, and more humane, way to apply technology to manufacturing. It was only then that they turned to a few brave visionaries who had been calling for a different approach. TQM was the product of that desperation. And, ironically, many of the techniques of CIM are finding productive use in modern companies . . . all they needed was the defining structure of total quality within which to operate.

Sales Force Automation is not yet in such dire straits. But its trajectory suggests a comparable fate. Yet, if we can learn from the story of TQM, we may spare ourselves that disaster. If we can develop a new, overarching philosophy like TQM that reverses the inhuman perspective of SFA, we may be able to preserve most of its tools while still achieving our goal of revolutionizing sales.

To begin that process, we must first turn our backs upon the demands of corporate management and focus our attention on the individual salesperson and his or her needs. And we can start with the exemplars, the salespeople who are already superproductive, and find out what they do right.

INFORMING THE SALESPERSON

A knowledgeable sales professional is a singular and powerful force in the marketplace—and a rare person to find. Knowledgeable, informed sales professionals are capable of engaging the customer in a high value-added selling process that multiplies their productivity compared to that of their professional peers.

What makes them special? A number of factors:

- A thorough understanding of their company's products and services, with an ability to explain the function, benefits, utility, and real cost, as well as correctly configure those products to a customer's needs;
- A perspective on the entire marketplace set in an historical context;
- A deep and subjective understanding of their customers'

desires, and how those needs have evolved over the
years;
- A practical knowledge of their competitors' products and
services and how they compare to their own;
- Immediate access to, or the ability to create on the spot,
relevant product information such as brochures, data
sheets, and catalogues;
- The ability to cite and exhibit industry studies, independent product evaluations, and relevant news stories and
feature articles;
- Skill at navigating around their own company to assure
on-time delivery, and superior service and support for
their customers throughout the life cycle of product use.

We have all met a few remarkable sales professionals
who exhibit many, if not all, of these characteristics. And
whenever we find such people we buy from them, we recommend them to our friends and associates, we follow
them from company to company; and when we can hire
them, we promote them. We write letters of commenda-
tion on their behalf. We latch on to them and we don't let
them go.

The individual described is the *informed salesperson*. Such
a personage used to be a product of chance, of serendipity.
Just as TQM proved that it is possible to take any manufacturing line and turn it into a top performer, so too is it possible, with the right perspective and the proper tools, to
turn any sales professional into an informed salesperson—
more knowledgeable, more resourceful, more responsive,
and ultimately more productive.

Moreover, these extraordinary performers need not be

lone wolves and corporate mavericks, but can be brought together into an *Informed Sales Force* that is even greater than the sum of its parts.

Such an Informed Sales Force is within our reach. The technology is available today. Time and distance are no longer obstacles. Only the will to implement remains a challenge.

When we turn the lens around and study the needs of the sales professional rather than those of the corporation, it quickly becomes obvious that what sales personnel need most is instant access to up-to-the-minute information—seamless, instant communication between sales, marketing, sales administration, and customer service. It also means a comprehensive marketing encyclopedia. A complete customer information system. A product information system. A market intelligence system. A competitive information system. Electronic product configuration and order processing. Proposal generation.

All of this can be done on a desktop, a laptop, even on a palmtop computer. And all of those individual devices can be networked to share information in real time throughout the organization. Imagine such a network, with every node focused upon adding value to the sales process, upon solving the customer's requirements . . . quickly, accurately and without error . . . and you get a sense of the power such an Informed Sales Force might have, and the added value it would bring to the corporation.

The Informed Sales Force is not a futurist's fantasy; it is realizable today. Some of the world's leading corporations—IBM, Hewlett-Packard, Pfizer, and Merck, among others—have already begun reaping the benefits of informing their sales forces. Sentry Market Research reports that "a majority of large organizations are re-engineering their sales processes and planning significant investments in platforms, networks, databases and sales automation software." Those that choose the right model—informing over automating—will have an unbeatable advantage over their competitors, big and small. For those companies that want to stay in the race, the only alternative is to start on the path to the Informed Sales Force now.

Where does that path start?

A good place is with the research of Barry Trailer of Sales Navigation Systems, Inc. Trailer has written, "In an effort to be proactive, managers often track activity. Believing in a 'The harder I work, the luckier I get' philosophy, they urge more sales calls, more proposals, etc."[7]

The result, says Trailer, is a crude sales equation of:

$$\text{Activity} = \text{Productivity}$$

In other words, the old sales funnel model. Trailer proposes a more realistic and compelling equation:

$$\frac{\text{Activity of sales force} \times \text{Quality of that activity}}{\text{Length of the sales cycle}} = \text{Productivity}$$

Note that Trailer's replacement equation adds a new variable to both the numerator and denominator. Increase the former or reduce the latter and you will radically improve sales productivity. Do both and productivity goes sky-high.

How do you do that? Well, reducing the sales cycle can be accomplished through a combination of better sales tools and by placing more control over the sales process, from configuration to contracts, in the hands of the individual salesperson. More on that in Chapter 8.

But what about that new variable, "quality," in the numerator? What does it mean? And how do we give it a value?

TOTAL SALES QUALITY

This chapter began with a discussion of a new application of technology, CIM, and how it has been undermined by a failed philosophy, automation. We saw how a similarly failed philosophy of automation is already undermining the important effort of bringing technology to sales. We then proposed a new model for sales technology: Virtual Selling and the Informed Sales Force.

But if automation is not the underlying dynamic of Virtual Selling, what is?

Return again to the lesson of manufacturing. Manufacturing technology finally realized its potential only after the general adoption of the Total Quality philosophy. TQM was implemented through the application of clear management direction, a retraining of the work force, the application of state-of-the-art information technologies, and a constant focus upon the customer. Most of all, whereas CIM was an open-ended model, TQM was *convergent*, it had the clear, identifiable goal of zero defects.

There is no reason to doubt that sales will be any different. Total Sales Quality (TSQ)—*the conversion of every qualified lead into a satisfied and ongoing customer*—is as realistic and salubrious a goal for the Informed Sales Force as Six Sigma quality is for manufacturing lines. And TSQ can be achieved the same way as TQM: through clear and consistent management direction, retraining the sales force, making full use of computer and telecommunications technologies, and keeping constant focus upon the customer.

Total Sales Quality (TSQ) will amount to a revolution in selling. Needless to say, getting there will require a re-engineering of the sales process. TSQ will change the way both sales professionals and their managers think. It will also dramatically change the way we sell and fundamentally alter the way we interact with each other and, more importantly, with customers.

Total Sales Quality will affect more than just the sales office. New demands will be placed on almost every other corporate operation as well. For example, marketing will be forced to provide perfectly focused, precisely targeted, thoroughly qualified sales opportunities. And these leads won't merely be traditional lists of company names and contacts either: rather, these "opportunities" will more resemble dossiers, corporate biographies. They will include a complete profile of account history, buying preferences, actual customer requirements, competitive products under evaluation, and scenarios predicting the outcome of different strategies. The salesperson will be able to ascertain the customer's buying intention and purchase time frame, as well as receive an explanation of any related products or services that the customer may have or require. The opportunity will explain the customer's preferred buying process, as well as how it intends to use the product. It will explain delivery requirements, financing requirements, and who the decision maker is. Purchase influencers will be outlined. It will reference friends and business associates of the prospect who are already customers.

In all, the sales opportunity will be a long way ahead of today's "leads list." In every way, it will live up to its name: each opportunity, if managed properly, will convert to a sale.

That's marketing. An informed salesperson needs context as well. And here the corporate IS function will be called upon to do its part. The sales professional will need instant and total access to product information, as well as market data, third-party evaluations, and all relevant new articles.

Manufacturing's relationship with sales will change, too, as the old rule that the sales force sells what the factory builds will be turned on its head. Now, increasingly, the customer will define the product and the factory's task will be to educate the sales professional to guide that customer within the realm of possibility.

Senior management will also be challenged. New metrics will need to be established to determine goals and commissions. New organizational schemes will be needed to deal with salespeople who are essentially independent intrapreneurs. Most of all, enormous amounts of trust will be required: management will have to give up much of the control that has always been its prerogative.

The vision of Total Sales Quality is that every sales presentation will be well focused and tailored to the customer's need. Every sales proposal will be precisely configured to match the customer's requirements. Each sales professional will be fully informed with the knowledge that he or she needs and empowered to generate product config-

urations precisely customized to the customer's unique requirements. And behind it all will be a comprehensive sales
information system that does more than just automate ex-
pense reports; it enables sales professionals to provide total
customer satisfaction.

The goal of Total Sales Quality is 100 percent success.
Just as Deming, Juran, and Crosby called for analyzing
each defective part to understand the underlying source of
its failure, so too in TSQ every miscued contact, misfit
lead, rejected proposal, or competitive loss must be scruti-
nized until the systemic cause of its failure is understood.
The process must then be modified to assure that that situation never occurs again.

In the early 1970s, TQM sounded as radical as TSQ
does today. But fifteen years from now we will look back,
and the very idea of generating 99 bad sales leads for every
one new customer will seem as ludicrous to us as throwing
out half of a factory's production.

Total Sales Quality is a belief in perfection—zero sales
defects, 100 percent lead quality, total customer satisfaction—and the success that comes from that perfection. As
we've said, the philosophy of Total Sales Quality is the
philosophical heart of the Informed Sales Force. And from
the Informed Sales Force comes loyal customers, increased
market share, a jump in sales productivity, and overall, a
thriving, growing, healthy business organization. To settle
for anything short of perfection is to accept failure—in
your products, in your people, in your processes, and finally and forever, in your company.

Chapter 3

Making the Sale

Why mess around with selling, throwing all sorts of electronic gewgaws at it with some foolhardy idea about making it work better? After all, sales is sales. It comes down to looking the customer in the eye and making that close. It's an art form whose rules never change: qualified leads, good merchandise, and a solid close. Put all three together and you'll be a rich man before you're forty.

And it's always been like that. Look at sales in literature. What are those real estate salesmen fighting over, even stealing, in *Glengarry Glen Ross?* Good leads and good products. Willy Loman? Good territory. Who was the Music Man? The King of the Close. If you believe Bruce Barton's 1925 best-seller *The Man Nobody Knows*, the art of selling was the same 2,000 years ago in Nazareth, and Jesus was the greatest salesman who ever lived.

So why tinker with selling now?

Making the Sale

We're not. We're trying to restore selling to what it is supposed to be—*selling.* Not filling out reports to the sales manager, not negotiating with corporate to get products delivered, not screaming at service for not getting a technician out to the customer site fast enough, not apologizing to the customer because headquarters can't deliver the upgrade it promised would be available now.

The simple fact is that, for the typical salesperson, the actual process of selling—what they joined the profession to do—is now down to a tiny fraction of the typical workday. The rest is corporate overhead. And that weight gets heavier every day.

Technology was the cause of much of this overhead, and it is to technology we must look for a way out. Thanks to computer networks, cellular telephones, fax machines, and e-mail, management, always suspicious of salespeople, has been able to expand its control over sales operations. In doing so management has made a crucial long-term strategic mistake. The field sales force, by resisting the imposition of many of these more onerous schemes, has often been blamed for holding back change—when in fact it has only been trying to preserve its independence and maintain the professional standards many of these corporations have lost.

Ironically, today some of the most forward-looking companies are reversing their early top-down decisions and converting that same technology to give more control to the individual salesperson. Thus, the salespeople are being vindicated.

But those cases are rare. Everywhere else, there is still a long way to go—and growing longer by the day. This chapter takes a look at all of the obstacles the typical modern corporation throws up in the path of its salespeople as they try to make a sale. You will no doubt recognize many of them . . . and taken all together they make a compelling case for change.

SALES PREVENTION

For all the articles and seminars and training sessions, the fact is that we in the business world do not know why certain people tend to be successful in sales. And frankly, we do little to find out.

Nor, from a corporate perspective, do we do much to understand and assist the sales process. We don't provide the proper tools, we do next to nothing to facilitate closure, and especially, we do little to create a well-engineered sales process that results in the creation of a satisfied customer. Were any other corporate department to suffer from this kind of neglect, there would be a mutiny—but in sales, it's all part of the business.

In the course of a typical workday, the situation is even more bleak. The very organizations assembled and financed to create the selling opportunity and assist the sales force are frequently perceived as, and in fact are, obstacles to the sales process. With good reason, salespeople usually see marketing and sales administrations as bloated, unfathomable institutions that are at best out of touch with the needs of the customer, and at worst actively trying to impede, even *prevent*, sales.

How bad is this "sales prevention"? Research suggests that even the best salespeople often can spend only a tiny

fraction of their work time actually focusing upon those relations with the customer that actually lead to sales—that
is, identifying good prospects, giving sales presentations,
configuring the order, and closing the sale. For even the
most disciplined salesperson the *majority* of the workday is
spent in bureaucratic overhead.

Even the most efficient, cutting-edge corporations are
little better. Take Oracle Corporation of Redwood Shores,
California, at $3 billion in annual sales one of the largest
and most successful computer software companies in
the world. Oracle is widely celebrated for the efficiency
and effectiveness of its sales force, a fact underscored
by the almost unprecedented growth of the company
since its founding in 1977. Yet, as the company itself will
admit, studies have found that its sales reps spend ap-
proximately half of their time wrestling orders through
corporate.

The cost of this inefficiency is breathtaking. Oracle, for
example, spends more than $750 million each year on sales
and marketing, nearly all of it on employee costs. Given
only 50 percent efficiency, that's $375 million in bungled
inefficiency—money that could instead be doubling Oracle's current profits. So why, with all of this inefficiency, is
Oracle thriving? Because everybody else in its industry is
in the same leaky boat. At its leading competitor, Sybase
Inc., across the Bay in Emeryville, sales reps spend on average *one week* wrestling with a single order through corporate.

What causes this delay in companies? Most of it is sales
prevention in its purest form: dragging an order through
the maze of corporate processes and with numerous incom-

patible information systems, wrestling with indifferent or hostile company bureaucrats, getting the order approved by managers who never seem to be around, cajoling manufacturing to build the product as configured and by the contracted date, correcting and recorrecting data entry errors, correcting billing errors, and lobbying to get the full and proper commission.

In the name of efficiency we have gotten ourselves into a very expensive mess. And there is no simple way out, because the objectives we have set and the incentives we employ only aggravate the situation rather than remedy it. Buying one more mainframe computer or 10,000 more portable telephones won't help us.

Instead, we have to take an honest look at the sales support functions—from lead generation to close, as well as training and tools—as they have been implemented in recent years . . . and not just from the perspective of Executive Row, but from that of the people on the ground: the sales manager, the sales reps, and the customers. We have to look past the promotion, the self-justification, and the delusion to see the real truth about modern sales.

LEAD GENERATION

Marketing's single most important objective is lead generation. For that purpose marketing was invented a century ago. The long-held objective is to get the sales pipeline filled with new potential sales opportunities and to do this on the most cost-effective basis. This in turn is believed to be the foundation for gaining market penetration and share, as well as for achieving revenue goals.

The process technology that has been developed over

the last one hundred years to support this strategy is Mass Marketing, the pseudo-science of reaching the largest number of potential consumers at the lowest possible cost. Mass marketing defines modern business, it is the heart of modern industrial life. Unfortunately, it is flawed at its very center.

The raw material of mass marketing is leads. As such, marketing is the "parts supplier" to sales. Its task is to get the sales process started. To do this, marketing must fill the leads pipeline with potential customers, then keep that pipeline regularly replenished.

Experience with this technique has shown that the use of mass marketing techniques—advertising, public relations, direct mail, collateral materials, point of sale promotions—produces lots of initial leads with a very small likelihood of an ultimate sale. In most industries that likelihood is on the order of less than 1 percent. At the aforementioned Oracle, it is 1000 leads per single sale . . . the 999 others are largely worthless.

As a result, the sales/marketing process resembles less a pipeline than a cone. This is the "sales funnel" we've already discussed. Within the sales funnel, the immense number of initial leads is narrowed down and culled out until at the focal point of the close only a handful pass through to become customers. And since the ratio of leads to sales appears to remain comparatively fixed, it is not surprising that the primary task of marketing is to widen the mouth of the funnel in order to create a commensurate increase in diameter at the spout. Thus, being incredibly optimistic, if 100 leads result in one sale, then 200 will yield two, 1,000 will yield ten, and 1,000,000 will get us 10,000 new customers!

An obvious problem with this, as any large company can tell you, is that of scale. If the ratio holds, then a large multinational corporation with, say 50,000 customers, must regularly churn through five million leads just to maintain itself. That is a mind-boggling organizational challenge as well as a huge waste of resources. Marketing departments are clogged with mountains of unqualified leads. Names, addresses, and phone numbers of trade show attendees, casual readers of company advertisements, watchers of commercials, people who absent-mindedly checked a box on a magazine coupon. Millions upon millions of leads . . . and few with any intention of ever buying the product. They don't need it. They can't possibly afford it. They've already bought something else. And yet each has to be contacted in some way to ascertain the magnitude of their indifference.

Trade shows, which consume vast corporate marketing budgets, are often the worst source of good leads. Attendees at these are the ultimate in tire kickers. Writes *Sales & Marketing Management*:

> Most exhibitors are unable to provide sales information regarding their trade show program, and the few who can consider the information unnecessary. This information gap has made it impossible to concoct a reliable formula that measures the return on sales from the expenditures of trade shows . . .
> . . . companies lure in trade show attendees by enticing crowds with gifts, raffles and even magical acts. Unfortunately, these gimmicks attract hordes of nonbuyers—and a lot of useless leads . . . [1]

Different companies react in different ways to this tsunami of leads. Some firms deal with the initial response entirely in the marketing department, typically by mailing back a product brochure or some equivalent. This can be an effective filter to get rid of the tire-kickers, but it also places the onus of any follow-up on the few truly motivated customers. *They* have the responsibility of making the effort to contact the sales organization—a step that goes against every model of successful selling.

By comparison, other, more progressive companies, wanting to empower their sales forces, do a quick division of the raw leads by territory and/or product line and distribute them directly to the reps. This gets the motivated leads through, but it also turns the reps into full-time qualifiers, forcing them to sort through stacks of names and addresses devoid of qualifying information or clues to buying intentions, demographic data, explanations of customer requirements, budget, time frame, account history, or just about anything else useful.

Neophyte salespeople will actually try to follow up on these leads in hopes of finding the needle in the haystack. Veteran reps know better and usually ignore the pile altogether. Either way, the motivated potential customer, despite being passed through to sales, is lost.

Such losses are painful for any company, and most are perpetually trying to find new ways to separate the few good leads from the multitudes of bad ones. Yet, this problem is minor compared to the much larger one that few companies ever address: *mass marketing doesn't really work.*

Mass marketing is built on the logical fallacy of extension, that is, the premise that ratios remain constant as scale increases. But we know that isn't true. Just because 100 leads result in one sale, there is no guarantee that 1 million leads will produce 10,000. On the contrary, there is every reason to believe that widening the mouth of the funnel only produces a fractional increase in the size of the spout. Here's why:

•*Market size:* Mass marketing is predicated on the axiom that the market universe is essentially infinite. In other words, you will never run out of potential customers. Now, while that may have been effectively true in 1890 or 1948, in our age of mass global communications it is no longer the case. Markets, no matter how large, are soon encompassed, and the wider a company reaches out for new leads, the more likely it is to reach beyond the boundaries of potential customers and go out into territory where no lead *ever* converts into a sale. That isn't likely to happen with a hundred leads, but it is very likely to happen with ten million.

•*Lead degradation:* Even if a company stays within the borders of its market, the quality of its leads is likely to degenerate over time. One reason for this is the simple rule of "cream-skimming": even the crudest mass marketing program is likely to capture the most motivated customers first, leaving an ever-diminishing pool of potential sales. A second reason is that the new corporations, with their need to build relationships and hold on to customers for a long time, will slowly bind up the best customers, often for years, eventually leaving only those potential customers that are hard to service, disloyal, or embittered. A third reason is that by throwing out one wide net after another, companies eventually hit individuals that are not currently potential customers, but may be at a future time. Unfortunately, these constant approaches can immunize those individuals to the pitch—a process that, ironically, affects good marketers better than bad marketers. Thus, when that individual is ready to become a customer, he or she may consider the message to be old news, or no longer hear it at all.

These factors argue that mass marketing won't stay constant with increased scale, but rather will see diminishing returns. The funnel widens but no longer achieves the expected gains. In response, the worried company widens it even more, using tools like Sales Force Automation software to expand the reach. But gains still fall short. And year after year the vicious cycle spirals on: more and more cheap, unfocused, unqualified leads, the overall quality diminishing as the quantity grows . . . and there seems no way out.

LEAD QUALIFICATION

In mass marketing, the fail-safe system for rapid lead generation is sophisticated lead qualification. Unfortunately, few companies know how to do it. Instead, as we have just noted, either they force the customer to qualify himself, or they rely upon each sales rep to do his or her own lead processing. In the case of the latter, this process is so time consuming and fraught with peril that lead qualification ability can become a primary determinant of a rep's sales productivity and long-term success.

To appreciate that, compare how differently a new salesperson and a successful veteran approach their respective mountains of raw leads. As we have said, the neophyte tackles the problem with sheer energy, following up on as many leads as possible, chasing down endless blind alleys before almost randomly chancing upon a real customer. Meanwhile, hiding in the remainder of the pile are other, now lost, sales.

By comparison, the very top salespeople know what to do with this raw material. They have an uncanny knack for quickly sorting through stacks of new leads to find a gem. Just watch one some time. The stack of trade-show leads instantly goes in the trash. They are a joke. So are bingo cards, and they get tossed too. Selecting the people who took the initiative to call or write in, the pro scans them quickly for a recognized account, a recognized name, perhaps a current customer. There's a possible: a lead bearing a rough explanation of the customer's requirements. Does it fit any company product? Yes. Keep it. Here's another, a handwritten note: "Customer intends to purchase this month, requests immediate call-back." Bingo. That lead stays on top of the desk.

Within minutes, the top salesperson has cut out 90 percent of the pile of leads he or she has been provided. They are all now in the trash, not worth the waste of a call. And, of the 10 percent that have made the cut, perhaps half will actually be contacted.

We have said that this sorting skill, perhaps more than any other, defines success. The 20 percent of the sales force that generates the 80 percent of the company's sales will inevitably share this talent. But then, that minority will always succeed no matter what obstacles the company throws before it.

Of much greater importance is the remaining 80 percent—the also-rans, some of them very skilled salespeople when in the right situation, but who are forever chasing worthless leads. They waste corporate resources, management time, and their own careers. They do this by following the instructions provided by their management. Improve their productivity just slightly—say, by increasing by 10 percent the quality of the leads they blindly chase, and the impact on the corporate balance sheet will be stunning.

But there is more wrong with contemporary lead qualification than the old 80/20 rule asserting itself. It has to do with the very definition of "qualification."

Even the most talented salespeople often see lead qualification as little more than that first cut between high- and low-probability sales prospects. They then rush off, cut the deal—and often miss the larger long-term opportunity that would come from an enduring customer relationship.

Conversely, many of those with limited culling skills understand that qualification is the process of interacting with the potential customer and gaining a thorough understanding of that customer's requirements, his decision process, purchase time frame, and purchasing history. Unfortunately, they are so busy chasing bad leads that they have little chance to display those skills. The result is that the entire sales force, both high and low producers, are typically operating well beneath their potential level of productivity.

This variability in skills continues to the actual interview with the customer. Each rep has his or her own stock set of questions—the information gathered may range from the cursory to the painfully detailed, and the resulting understanding may be sketchy or encyclopedic. Here again, it is very possible that yet a third, distinct, segment of the sales force may be weak in the first two disciplines, but be gifted at this third one. Unfortunately, these salespeople rarely get to the interview step, and when they do, they don't know how to convert the rich information they've gained into a long-term sales relationship.

So, when we look at a typical sales force, what we really see is not the traditional, and simplistic, dualism of good and bad salespeople, but instead *three* categories of salespeople: those who can sift leads, those who can quickly understand the customer, and those who can establish a long-term relationship with that customer. We reward the first, and punish the other two for wasting half their time unproductively. And yet, for the long-term needs of the modern corporation—lifelong customers, consumer coproduction, etc.—the latter two skills may actually be more important.

Of course, if we had a lead-generation system that really worked, a lead-qualification system as efficient as our top salespeople, and a way of spreading information around the organization so that the unique skills of our "other" salespeople were put to work, we might have radically more productive, competitive, and profitable companies than we have now. But needless to say, the mass marketing system is not set up for such a new order, and the fancy new Sales Force Automation software programs are ultimately designed only to reinforce the status quo. Instead, the preponderance of salespeople are punished for not having the right skill set, and the useful information they gather and the important relationships they have built are tossed away. Meanwhile, we subsidize the notion of sales as a quick, one-time hit, while the knowledge we've gathered, which cost us more than half our sales and marketing budget to generate, collect, and refine, is thrown away.

But who cares? After all, we'll never run out of customers, will we?

LEAD TRACKING

Once we manage, somehow, through this confused generation process to actually locate a real, bona fide, potential customer for our product, what do we do with the information? How do we manage it? How, assuming that it will be passed through several hands before actual contact is made, do we track that lead through the organization? How and when do we follow up? Or do we follow up at all? Or does the lead get detained or lost in the corporate bureaucratic labyrinth, never to be seen again—or does it reappear, like a misplaced love note in a novel, long after the initial ardor has faded and the suitor has gone off to marry someone else?

In recent years, as part of the Sales Force Automation "revolution" (revanchement, more properly), companies have invested billions of dollars in computer networks specifically designed to track sales leads through their organizations. And it is a measure of how successful those investments have been that, here in the 1990s, the most popular lead-tracking technology remains the *back of the business card.*

After all that money spent on client-server systems, hard-wired communications networks, optical character readers, laser printers, and all of the other effluvia of the computer age, the most common—and if popularity is a clue, most efficient—lead-tracking system in most companies is ten cryptic words scribbled on three square inches of white, heavy stock paper.

If you don't believe that, walk through any sales department and look at how salespeople actually manage information. There are stacks of business cards and scraps of paper everywhere. Wallets are stuffed with business cards, as is the top drawer of the desk at the office and the dresser at home. So is the glove compartment of the car. Customer-product requirements are written on the backs of envelopes. Organization charts, half smeared from months of being brushed with passing sleeves, are written on whiteboards.

In other words, despite the expensive computer system glowing malevolently down the hall, nothing has changed in a half century. Willy Loman, once he got used to touch-tone phones and the absence of hats, would feel right at home.

. . . Actually, that isn't quite true. There *has* been one new technology—the most important to sales in the last half century—that has transformed the profession forever. This invention has become the centerpiece of every salesperson's daily working life, and without it, many careers would quickly grind to a halt.

No, not the personal computer. Not the cellular telephone either. It is the Post-it™ Note. Yellow ones and pink ones. The Post-it™ Note is a product of genius because it is essentially a business card that stays wherever you put it. On the wall. On the phone. On the address book. To date, in most sales offices, the most important application found for the laptop computer is as a portable carrier of Post-it™ Notes.

Thus, in the end, after we have spent vast sums to locate and qualify potential customers, and spent even greater fortunes to gather information on those customers, we then take this information and scatter it to unretrievable locations throughout the firm, storing it on ephemeral scraps of sticky paper. We have no effective means of storing this information centrally within the company. We have no organized means for retrieving and reusing it. And if this information does not immediately result in a sale, it is probably lost forever. Forget the computers. *This* is the real state of the art.

On the positive side, unlike computers, where obsolete and wrong information tends to survive forever, poisoning all future relations with the customer, the business card/Post-it™ Note system of lead tracking is self-purging: eventually the business card gets lost in the bottom of the desk drawer, and the Post-it™ Note curls up and falls to the floor, where the janitor sweeps it away.

SALES PRESENTATION

Now we come to the real "art" in selling: the presentation to the customer.

Once again, as with every such personalized step in the sales cycle, the 80/20 rule goes into effect. A fraction of the professionals in a given sales department have the verbal improvisational skills required to get in front of a group of near strangers and not only make a sales presentation, but, on the fly, in the face of unexpected questions, modify and customize that presentation in real time. And, once again, these facile and quick-thinking individuals are not always the same ones who can perform well the other steps of the sales process.

Moreover, being clever in sales presentations also brings with it a whole new set of problems. For one thing, as is often celebrated in the mythology of sales, legendary sales presentations are often built on bluff and bravado. The gifted salesperson, sensing that the customer might not be content with the company's offerings, abandons the catalogue and offers the moon and the sun—betting that he or she can cover the bet later either by jiggering up something from the factory or by converting the customer to a more feasible configuration.

Either way, the customer ends up with a product or service it didn't expect and doesn't really want . . . and either goes somewhere else in the future or becomes one of those unsatisfied customers that forever haunts and hectors the organization. Needless to say, neither result is what strong, enduring companies are built on. Meanwhile, the clever salesperson, having constructed this Ponzi sales scheme on misrepresentation, begins spending more and more time trying to control an ever-mounting pile of false promises. Productivity falls and the company burns up resources coping with angry customers and their misinformed expectations.

And these are the *successful* sales. What do the other 80 percent of salespeople do? They make up for the freewheeling, high-risk techniques of the elite salespeople by giving presentations that are the sales equivalent of forcing the complex, rounded needs of the customers into a single square hole. These presentations, *sales sermons,* you might call them, are inflexible, rote, and most commonly consist of the salesperson indulging in a few standard personal interactions (How about those Knicks? Is that a photo of your family?) before launching into a verbatim reading of the bulleted points from a marketing proposal or the section titles of a product brochure. Customer questions, of course, are frowned upon.

Deadly stuff, and hardly conducive to selling the customers. But managers love sales sermons precisely because they preclude creativity by the sales force. After all, they say to themselves, if those clowns will just stick to the script and not go off the reservation and start making wild claims and promises, then I won't have to take calls from angry customers, and an even angrier factory. In other words, the best sales strategy is the one least likely to make waves. Or to work.

Of course, there is another way. That would be to use the new multimedia technology to create dynamic and exciting presentations that would both entertain and enlist the customer, while at the same time remaining constrained by the configurations available in the company catalogue. With such tools, the clever seller would be reined in, but not crushed; while the less eloquent sales professional would be buoyed up by the high quality of the presentation itself. Meanwhile, the customer would become a participant in the product configuration, learn all of the company's capabilities, and be secure in the knowledge that the order will be met and delivered.

But, of course, to do that would require putting even

more control in the hands of the sales force, giving sales-people even more independence. No more sales sermons. And what manager would ever allow that to happen?

SALES FULFILLMENT

Sales fulfillment, in case you haven't encountered the term, is the process of providing customers and prospects with the product literature and documentation that they need to fully understand a product or service and how it applies to their needs.

One reason you may never have heard the term is that in many companies the process never actually reaches the individual salesperson and the client it is supposed to "fulfill." Instead, the huge mass of materials gets halfway down the ever-narrowing distribution pipe until finally the system clogs up and the entire enterprise suffers information constipation.

As with many executive programs, sales fulfillment begins with a sincere effort to help sales . . . and ends up becoming yet one more obstacle in the path of the sales force.

Every year, corporate marketing departments spend billions of dollars working to arm their salespeople with support documents that fully address customer questions and concerns. Armies of copywriters, graphic artists, photographers, printers, video producers, and editors spend millions of man-hours generating a tsunami of collateral marketing materials: brochures, product catalogs, videotapes, data sheets, reprinted trade press articles and reviews, competitive evaluations, customer success stories, and on and on.

Making the Sale

And each time a new product is introduced the height of that wave of materials is multiplied. Thus, in a big corporation, such as Texas Instruments or Motorola, where products number in the thousands, the number of collateral documents multiply by the tens of thousands. Just keeping track of these documents is its own inventory challenge. At General Electric, a total marketing staff of over 10,000 employees produces thousands of collateral materials each year: multiply that by print runs of 100,000 or more each and (to the sound of whole forests falling) GE has become one of the largest publishers in America, as big as McGraw-Hill. Just storing all of this printed matter fills up a score of giant warehouses scattered throughout the country. And that's just for GE's U.S. operations.

Again, all of this is meant to help. But the reality is that if all of this material actually *did* reach sales, that operation would be overwhelmed. The typical salesperson would be paralyzed trying to stay abreast of the deluge of collateral goods. Fortunately (or unfortunately) the internal distribution system of most companies is so lousy that most of this marketing stuff never even gets to the salesperson, but molders away in some warehouse until it can be recycled into something useful.

The reason for this distribution failure is obvious: say your company has 100 sales offices employing 1,000 salesperson selling 100 products. Now, just to be conservative, say that each of those products has generated 10 collateral documents. That means, to keep each of those salespeople fully supplied, you would not only have to print *one million* items (and many companies do), but deliver them, in collated lots of 10,000 each, to 100 geographically diverse locations. Given a two-year life cycle for most modern products, you would have to replace half a million documents per year, making sure that the obsolete versions are properly disposed of.

Now, leaving aside the obvious problem of how to store this paper blizzard at the average sales office, just the challenge of such a distribution system would be enough for most companies to take on as their primary business—much less try to attempt it while still actually making and distributing products. So, instead, they just *pretend* it all works and try not to look too closely. And that is a pity, because within those reams of documents are items that are both compelling and uniquely targeted to specific customers. Unfortunately, outside of the people who created them, few in the company even know these documents exist.

We all know what really happens instead. Salespeople get accustomed to a few brochures and data sheets that they find useful and just keep reordering them. When heading out on a call, they swing by the storage closet in the sales office and grab a handful that might have something to do with the customer. Grab as many as possible too, no matter how limited the connection, because it is better to err on the side of overkill.

And, when these collateral items become grossly obsolete or in short supply, these same salespeople become adept at using the revolutionary invention that is only second to the Post-it™ Note in its impact on sales: the copier. A man or woman with a good eye and steady hands can make hundreds of copies of a particularly positive review or interesting brochure . . . and, with a little cutting and pasting, you can excise all of those pesky sections that no longer fit the company's profile.

Of course, a custom cover letter with these materials is always an effective touch. But that's out of the question. In a world of two-finger-typing salespeople, letter generation takes too much time. That is, except for that smooth-talking 20 percent elite. With pleas, solicitations, threats, and flirtations, they can usually convince some administrative assistant to type the letter—again improving their productivity. Everybody else does without, at best scratching some cliché ("Give me a call!") on their attached business card.

PROPOSING A SOLUTION

If, after all of this abuse, misdirection, and neglect, the potential customer is still interested, the salesperson must then generate a proposal that offers a product configuration to help that customer achieve a *solution*—if ever a word was so misused—to its problem.

This process involves two distinct, but related, activities. The first is *generating a proposal*. This may sound daunting, what with all of the requirements and documentation demanded by the customer, but, as most readers who are salespeople know, it is actually quite easy. That's because nobody ever actually produces a customized proposal. Organizations hate that kind of liberty by salespeople, so they typically make the process into an administrative nightmare requiring sign-offs and official approval and review and anything else they can think of to signal to the salesperson that he or she has made a terrible, terrible mistake and must never, ever do such a thing again. This, of course, changes with very large contracts. There, because every petty corporate bureaucrat wants to claim credit, getting help in customizing the proposal is usually pretty easy.

Instead, the goal is to *give the illusion* of a customized proposal while using the standard, and thus safe, company proposals.

Here, at last, is where we finally come to a real-life application where computers have helped sales productivity. With a PC and a good laser printer you can stitch together the best stuff from several past approved proposals, using the search-and-replace function to change names and product numbers . . . and still have the final result look like it is a professional production created just for that customer.

The second, parallel, activity is *product configuration.* In most companies this term is actually an oxymoron, because one of the first things a new salesperson learns—usually from a voice screaming over the telephone—is that all company products are nonconfigurable. As with custom proposals, a custom product solution is not only out of the question, but even suggesting it is a punishable offense.

Learning this fact can be a painful experience, but once you do, the task before you becomes crystal clear: your job is not to sell the customer what it needs, but to convince the customer to want what you've got. This is best accomplished by a triple combination of attacking your competitor, confusing the customer as to its real needs, and overselling your own company's products.

And it works. Of course, a few months down the line the

customer, faced with a purchase that doesn't do the job and realizing it has been suckered, may become a bit annoyed. But that is customer service's problem. You got your commission.

CLOSING THE SALE

It was the great military strategist von Clausewitz who noted that war was not a separate enterprise, but a continuation of politics by other means. So too, as we look at the sales process up to this point, we realize that the close is not a separate activity, but is the inevitable result of what came before. In fact, one can argue that the traditional close is, as it is often described, an "art" precisely because it takes nimble footwork and a large bag of tricks to overcome all of the misadventures that preceded it.

Look at it from the customer's point of view. To get to this point the potential purchaser has likely had his initial request for information ignored for several weeks, then been sent a stack of mostly irrelevant materials, sat through a standard presentation that had little to do with the solution he needs, then been handed a proposal that doesn't quite fit what he asked for. Not surprisingly, he is having second thoughts about the deal—and his experiences with your company to date have made him dubious about your extravagant promises of service and support to come.

Well, there's only one answer. *Ya gotta trick 'em.* There are a number of ways to coerce or manipulate a customer into a sale—and the reader has probably been taught most of them. Get him saying yes until he can't say no. Cozy up to him and pretend you're his friend. Promise anything. And when all else fails, bring in senior management for the brute force approach. Flatter him and at the same time strike into him the fear of God. Have your legendary CEO shake his hand and tell him how important this relationship is, while at the same time mentioning how he, the CEO, is golf buddies with the customer's boss's boss's boss.

Of course, this kind of emotional mugging can have some pretty ugly aftereffects, but then again, that's not your problem.

PLACING THE ORDER

The sale closed, the contract signed, the customer wondering what just hit him, the victorious salesperson now encounters the next great oxymoron: *sales administration*. Such a phrase suggests the cool and competent management of the passage of a new sales order through the organization, from the sales office to the factory to the customer. It doesn't quite capture the chaos, random motion, infighting, politicking, and the incompetence that truly characterizes the process in most companies.

The first thing to understand is that in most companies order tracking is still largely a manual process. The scientists over in your company's R&D lab may be designing new products in color 3-D on $50,000 workstations, but your order is most likely inching its way through the organization on a sheet of xeroxed paper. And that's when it's moving. Most of the time it sits in managers' in-boxes awaiting approval before it can move on.

Then, at various points, such as when it arrives at the

factory and when the resulting product is packaged to be shipped, the order is rewritten. That is, it is retyped onto a new format to get it through the next bureaucratic stage. In large organizations, the order may be retyped half a dozen times. The result is something like the childhood game of Post Office: every time another clerk retypes that order the odds increase that an error is being introduced: a wrong address, ZIP code, part explosion number, location code, etc.

Even if the odds are only ten to one of this occurring during a particular re-entry, after six or seven of these exchanges the chances are that *most* orders will now contain some inaccuracies. That is why some famous corporations, surveying their internal tracking systems, have been stunned to find that *100 percent* of their orders are initially unshippable.

You know what happens next: the customer, already having second thoughts about the deal, doesn't get his or her order on time. Or it is misconfigured. Or it is sent to the wrong place. Whatever the screw-up, all of his doubts are now confirmed. And the customer goes nuts, calling the salesperson and screaming threats to either cancel the order or sue.

Now it is the salesperson who has been hung out to dry. He or she suddenly has visions of commissions, in the form of winged hundred-dollar bills, flying out to sea. And now, often for the first time, the customer and the salesperson build a relationship out of a common cause: *to get justice from the company.*

Overtly or, more often, covertly, the salesperson now becomes an enemy of his or her employer, an insurgent pitted against the company to achieve an opposing goal. And different salespeople have different guerrilla techniques. Some just yell "Fire!," broadcasting urgent e-mails throughout the organization to create constructive panic. The smartest salespeople cultivate contacts at choke points throughout the organization that they can contact when they need to keep things moving—even to circumvent rules or leapfrog other orders. For these hustlers the system can be made to work—though often at the cost of other, more important orders.

But whatever technique the salesperson uses to force an order through a dyspeptic corporation, typically it consumes 70 percent or more of his or her time. Combine that with all of the other bureaucratic hassles thrown at that salesperson, and then add all of politicking, begging, and wheedling needed to get a fair commission check delivered before the next mortgage payment, and we are now looking at a typical salesperson spending as much as *90 percent* of his or her time *not* selling.

That leaves just 10 percent of the average workday—48 minutes in an eight-hour day—to actual *selling*, what that individual does best, what he or she got into the business to do and was trained for, and most of all, what creates the revenues of that corporation.

REVENUE FORECASTING

Given a workforce that is allowed to do its real job each day for an interval shorter than it is given for lunch, that chases mountains of false leads, that is given little useful information about the customer, that is forced to coerce or manipulate the customer into a sale and then must shepherd the subsequent order through the organization to keep it from being lost or screwed up, it should not be surprising that when asked by management to predict the likelihood of upcoming sales, sales management usually cannot (or will not) come up with a realistic projection.

How can it? The whole process is so volatile, unpredictable, and surreal, so dependent upon rumor, bravado, and the unexpected, that salespeople can't help but predict impending deals that suddenly vanish, or discount opportunities that suddenly pan out. Multiply this inexactness by several hundred salespeople and it is no wonder that overall projections made by sales management to Executive Row are almost never matched by reality—which creates surpluses or shortages in inventory, lost sales opportunities, and misapplication of capital. In fact, the whole sales projection process often becomes indistinguishable from black magic, with sales management struggling to find auguries of the future by rummaging through the entrails of recent orders, office gossip, and the hunches of the top salespeople.

Faced with this essentially impossible task, many sales managers take a cue from their people and try to get by with a combination of bluff and bravado. Like multiple sets of books. And projections so qualified as to be meaningless—that are then met by stealing sales from the next measurement cycle.

Meanwhile, the endless struggle to find even vaguely realistic projections forces these same managers to spend most of their time interrogating the salespeople to determine the status of their accounts, rather than helping them to become more productive.

But then, there is a certain poetic symmetry in this. In the modern corporation, the sales force spends most of its time not selling, and sales management spends most of its time not helping them do so.

SALES TRAINING

So, how do we help the sales force do its job? *Training,* of course. It's a multibillion-dollar industry.

Sales training comes in several guises. For the newly hired salespeople, or for veteran staffers being trained in a new technology, there is the standard one-week introductory program. As everyone who has been through one of these training sessions knows, they usually involve force-feeding the poor salespeople more information than they can possibly assimilate in the shortest possible time—a process captured in the vivid phrase "drinking from a fire hose." The poor salesperson, who is usually still trying to understand what the product *does,* is quickly swept along into arcane discussions about power supplies, firmware, and plasma displays. And, because the flow of information is always one way, the "students" are never given the opportunity to express their ignorance and ask for help.

Marshall Cox, one of the pioneers in the selling of integrated circuits, relates that he arrived at his first meeting at Fairchild Semiconductor in 1960—and spent the entire day listening to lectures about field-effect transistors without ever being able to figure out whether the giant four-foot computer chip projected on the screen was being shown actual size or blown up from microscopic. Afterwards, he joined the others at the company's traditional Scotch and brownie party and consumed those victuals until he didn't care about his question anymore.

It is to the credit of many companies that in the intervening years they have learned that their new salespeople have trouble remembering much (actually, any) of what is thrown at them at these sessions. So, as back-up, they send the salespeople off with what is usually three 3-inch-thick notebooks containing product materials that are equally incomprehensible, but have the added benefit of being organized incoherently. Finally, to make absolutely sure that no one has learned anything, companies take great pains not to pretest, posttest, or in any way measure skills acquisition.

A better-known training event is the annual company sales meeting. This is ostensibly a gathering to inform and motivate the sales force about new products to come and to help it better sell those products that are here now. But in reality annual sales meetings have one or two real purposes: they are either celebrations or political forums.

Celebratory sales meetings are usually thrown at resorts and are great fun. It's like a giant frat party: you get drunk, raise hell, and dance on the beach. You also learn nothing and, in terms of company revenues, accomplish nothing. But, of course, this enormous waste of time is justified because such gatherings are seen as "good for morale"—as if a week of bacchanalian fun makes up for 51 weeks of on-the-job misery and frustration.

With political sales meetings you don't even get the fun. This type of meeting usually is the result of top management seeing one too many photos of drunken salespeople having fun in silly costumes, photos that confirm all of their suspicions about the sales department, and demanding that these meetings become sober instructional events. Instead, with no recreational outlets available, they quickly disintegrate into court intrigue, with the more ambitious salespeople using the time to suck up to the boss and jockey for the next promotion—while everybody else stands around like wallflowers at a high-school dance, seething with envy at their more facile peers. That—plus several days of being stuffed with information, a couple more unreadable notebooks, and several verses of the company song—and everybody is happy as hell to get back to the old job rut.

THE SALESMAN'S TOOLKIT

So here we are. We are now nearly a half century into the electronics age, perhaps the greatest transformation in work and the tools of work that mankind has ever experienced in a single lifetime.

It is now possible to sit at a desk or in a car, and with the tap of a few fingers, access almost all of the world's knowledge. We can watch 500 channels of television, or construct television programs of our own. We can telephone people and see their faces as they speak to us. We can model the most complicated designs imaginable and then watch them operate, without ever having to actually build them or risk lives testing them. We can look inside a living brain, then reconstruct it in three dimensions on a television screen. We can transmit volumes of text and color images to any place in the world in a matter of seconds.

And yet, when we look at the daily life of a typical salesperson, we search in vain for any of the effects of this revolution. Here, in summary, is the standard salesperson's toolkit in the 1990s:

Making the Sale

- *Contact Information System:* What the salesperson can keep in his head or on Post-it™ Notes.
- *Product Information System:* A stack of out-of-date, marked-up, or photocopied brochures.
- *Competitive Information System:* Three outdated pages from the marketing department and a copy of the competitor's brochure.
- *Personal Information System:* A Day-Timer.
- *Configuration Management System:* A photocopied price list with handwritten updates.
- *Proposal Generator:* The copying machine.

This is both shocking and depressing. Where a universe of useful information should be at the salesperson's fingertips, instead he or she is flying blind. Where the salesperson should be directing the sales process, he or she is at the mercy of it. And where the salesperson should be the customer's advocate, he or she is instead the customer's partner in subterfuge.

We began this chapter by asking: Why now, of all times, should we be seeking to transform the profession of selling? As the pages that followed have shown, the simplest answer is that *we have no choice.* Selling is no longer hitting the pavement and flogging a half dozen simple products and then sending in the order. Now it is pitching ten thousand products of mind-numbing complexity to customers scattered throughout the globe. Worse, the technological revolution that has transformed the rest of the company has created an aggressive and sometimes malignant infrastructure that is rapidly eating away at the salesperson's real job of selling. In other words, sales *must* change *if only to save itself.*

Perhaps worst of all, the new tools being offered to help sales protect itself often turn out to do just the opposite: they make the sales force even more vulnerable to the predations of the corporate bureaucracy. They are gasoline cans disguised as fire extinguishers.

Is there a better solution? Yes, but it requires its own revolution; one that begins with a complete reversal in perspective. And to do that, we must start again at the beginning, with the technology itself, and rethink how can it liberate rather than oppress. That's the subject of the next chapter.

But will it work? Yes, and we believe this because we know salespeople. In spite of all of the obstacles thrown up by the modern corporation to prevent the process, salespeople still manage to find the good lead, make the sale, and close the deal.

Just imagine what they could accomplish if we actually helped them . . .

Chapter 4

The Hurried Pace of Change

In June 1994, in a tiny six-inch story, *Sales & Marketing Management* magazine carried the announcement by MO-V Inc. of Zeeland, Michigan, of a new mobile sales office for, in the magazine's words, "today's road warriors."[1]

Calling it "the perfect solution for people who need an office, but also need to stay out in the field," Chuck Lippert, MO-V president, showed off a Chevrolet Astro EXT van equipped with a desk complete with high-density filing, ergonomic swivel chair, and task light, IBM-compatible 486 notebook computer, desktop inkjet printer, fax machine, cellular phone, and hands-free/remote telephone usable as far as 1,000 feet from the van. The entire package could be leased for less than $600 per month.[2]

What makes the MO-V mobile sales office van interesting is not that it is remarkable, but that it is not. Twenty years ago, the sight of such a van would have struck by-standers dumb, as if they'd seen an invader from Mars. Now, such a rig likely passes unnoticed, yet one more prosaic part of the technological fabric of modern life. The richest tycoon in the world could not have built the MO-V in 1975; today the average salesperson can rent it for the cost of a few business dinners per month.

Even more amazing, there were no doubt many readers of the article who asked, "Why just a 486 notebook computer? Why not a Pentium?" Or who were disappointed that the printer was just an inkjet, not a laser. They also might have asked why there was no copier, or why the fax machine wasn't simply built into the computer, or why there wasn't a satellite dish on the roof for teleconferencing.

Such is the nature of the electronics revolution.

Perhaps most telling of all are the words of one MO-V customer, Jeff Brown, an agent manager with US Cellular who uses the van three or four days per week. He told the magazine, "If somebody can't see me right away, then I can just go outside to work in my office until they're ready."[3] Brown, it seems, far from being overwhelmed by the technological marvel under his control, saw it as merely another tool for getting the daily job done—and, more important, had already used it to reconstruct his business day.

When we talk about the technological revolution igniting sales, we often forget that to some degree that revolution has already been going on for nearly thirty years. The difference is that we are no longer startled by—or terrified of—technological marvels. Rather, we quickly assimilate them into our lives and incorporate them into our careers.

The Hurried Pace of Change

From digital telephones to voice mail, cellular phones to word processing, video cassettes to teleconferencing, nothing coming down the technological pipe, no matter how remarkable, can be any more stunning or dislocating than what we have already encountered.

Though in large measure the life of a typical salesperson is little changed from fifty years ago, on closer inspection one can see everywhere the deep beachheads made by technology. If we don't recognize this fact, it is often because we too have assimilated those innovations and they have lost their capacity to surprise. Yet each day the typical salesperson uses a personal computer, leaves phone-mail messages on a digital telephone recorder, places a call on a cellular telephone, sends a facsimile, copies presentational materials on a personal copier, answers a pocket pager and perhaps prints an overhead slide presentation on a laser printer. *None* of these products existed for everyday use even a decade ago. Now they are common sales productivity tools.

The MO-V is just one example of how sales has already assimilated advanced technology, and in the process has been transformed by it. Even a simple survey of the business press uncovers scores more; for example:

•At Vulcan Binder & Cover, a Vincent, Alabama-based division of EBSCO Industries Inc. that sells ring binders and other presentational materials, the sales department has been reorganized to take advantage of a new computerized marketing and sales management system. Until 1991 when the system was installed, according to Charles Neece, Vulcan's telesales manager, salespeople regularly kept track of leads and accounts on desk calendars and handwritten call-sheets. Average cost per call was approaching $400.[4]

By installing the system—an IBM AS/400 computer with Marketing Information Systems software—Vulcan saw a jump in telemarketing sales of 20 percent in just three months. On the field sales side, customer contacts more than doubled from 50 to 120 per day, with a commensurate increase in leads. Meanwhile, telesales maintained its efficiency with only half the staffing in outbound callers.

Moreover, the quality of these contacts was vastly increased. For example, in one of the first assignments for the new system, Neese asked for a list of all customers who hadn't purchased within the preceding 15 months. To his amazement, Neese found that these customers weren't lost, merely changed: "In ninety percent of the cases, the reason was that there'd been a change in decision makers. As a result, we'd simply stopped contacting the company.[5] Needless to say, those losses were quickly reversed.

The quality of the contacts was also improved by using the computer for customizing, and personalizing, the interchange with Vulcan. Salespeople now could work from 80 different basic letters, which they could modify directly on the computer screen. A telemarketer or salesperson could now call up a customer's complete sales history with Vulcan—thus both personalizing future contacts and improving customer satisfaction. Customers' birthdays were even added to the database, so that now each customer received a handwritten birthday greeting on his or her special day.

But as important as these changes were to Vulcan's bottom line, an even more profound effect could be seen in the

The Hurried Pace of Change

daily operations of the sales department. Both salespeople and telemarketers were initially wary of sharing any of their proprietary customer information with their peers. This wariness had long been the cause of lost sales to Vulcan, as potential leads dropped into the gap between territories or were handled by the wrong operation.

Part of this fear was answered by the software itself, which separated access-to-customer files between those users who could only look at the data, those who could use it, and those who could change it. Thus, the telesales people could only *look* at a salesperson's customer file, not touch it.

But the system didn't merely assuage this fear; more importantly, it rendered it meaningless. According to *Sales & Marketing Management*:

> At its best . . . the system feeds leads of such high quality to field salespeople and telesales reps that deals are closed on the first call, effectively reducing the sales cycle to near zero. Better still, there's little danger of telesales and field sales tripping over each other. When a qualifier enters a new lead into the system, the computer automatically matches the zip code against existing field territories. If the territory isn't covered by the field, the lead goes to telesales. Otherwise, the system automatically routes the information to the appropriate field salesperson and responds to the prospect with a fax (in the salesperson's name) telling them to expect a call.[6]

In other words, if highly qualified leads are coming as fast as you can handle them, who has time to worry about feuding over territory with the guys down the hall?

Not surprisingly, this new flow of information soon began to transform the organization of Vulcan's sales as well. In telesales, Neese's department, the operation was restructured to two qualifiers handling cold calling, nine outbound telesales reps (half the previous staffing, the rest dropped by attrition), eight stock people to take orders, and ten coordinators to support field sales. In field sales, these economies, combined with ever-increasing sales success, allowed for the hiring of six more salespeople, bringing that department's staff to thirty-four.

•Physician Sales & Service (PSS), a Jacksonville, Florida, distributor of medical equipment, pharmaceuticals, and supplies, credits a $1.5 million investment in Compaq portable computers and RAM Mobile Data wireless networking with increasing its sales more than $170 million in just four years. In the meantime, says Darlene Kelly, the company's vice president of information technology, "The investment paid for itself in less than a year."[7]

In the past, Kelly told *Sales & Marketing Management*, order entry:

> . . . was a bottleneck in our organization. The salesperson had to call in the order, and when you have one person in the field talking to one or two people in the home office the process takes a long time. Also, reps often spend time looking for a phone or fax line. We wanted to make it easier for reps to process orders as fast as possible so we could give our customers same day delivery instead of the two days it used to take.[8]

The Hurried Pace of Change

These days, in the course of a typical schedule that includes 200 accounts visited once every two weeks, a PSS salesperson can take a physician's order and process it on the spot, even answer doctor inquiries. Most important, the wireless in-field processing has freed as much as eight hours per week of additional selling time per rep. As purchasing decisions by doctors are more and more decided by their professional relationships with each sales rep, those added hours, Kelly believes, are vital to increased sales . . . a belief supported by PSS's recent performance.

•For the 52 sales reps in the golf division at Wilson Sporting Goods, the Chicago-based sporting goods giant, the work week always began miserably on Sunday.[9] That was the day when the reps had to download into their personal computers from Wilson's big mainframe computer all of the relevant financial and product information—general account, customer information, inventory data—that they would need for the subsequent week.

The process would take as long as two hours by modem, during which time they would have to hover nearby to make sure the telephone connection didn't skip a beat or go down. Complained one salesman, "I would usually have to babysit my laptop to make sure it was properly downloading."[10]

Yet, despite all of this, typically most of this mountain of new data would already be old, obsolete, even wrong, by the following Friday, as customer orders changed inventory amounts and sales prospects.

Frustrated, Wilson's management information department in July 1993 went out in search of a better solution. They found it in wireless data communications, a technology that uses a radio frequency to transmit large volumes of data through a process, called packet switching, that is both cheaper and more reliable than, say, cellular telephones.

The system Wilson put into place combined Motorola modems, which could be attached to each rep's laptop computer, with the Ardis wireless data network of 1,250 radio base stations. Total cost: about $170 per month per rep, little more than the old cost of batch downloading from the big computer.

Now Wilson Golf reps, wherever they are, from the office to a customer site, can instantly call up the latest sales and financial information from the home office—and, conversely, update that data for their peers. They can even receive order confirmations by fax to their laptop.

Says Mike Augur, the rep who used to "babysit" his laptop: "Since the information is always at my fingertips, I am able to give my customers immediate attention."[11] Adds his boss, national sales manager Dave Jensen, "It's hard to put a price on what it does for the reps in terms of image enhancement."[12]

•In a case of *literally* using technology to create a "field" sales force, the Monsanto Company's agricultural operation worked with software maker Pharos Technologies Inc. to develop a soil and crop management system for farmers based on the Apple Newton personal digital assistant.

The Infielder Crop Records System, as the product is called, uses internal software in the Newton, as well as

The Hurried Pace of Change

satellite communications, to enable farmers to develop crop strategies, obtain the latest commodity pricing news, and track soil conditions. Future software for the system will enable a farmer to call up satellite data on a given property to determine what chemical treatment it might need for a given crop.[13]

What does Monsanto gain from this? Farmers using the Infielder will be able to order goods from the company right from the field. Says Lou Clark, Monsanto's director of technical development, "When you are out in the field, there are a lot of decisions to be made [on the spot]. It may be awfully nice if you were in the field and could order products."[14]

And, needless to say, by converting individual farmers into their own retail salespeople, Monsanto increases the productivity of its own in-house sales force by freeing it to focus on large-order accounts.

Like the MO-V story, each of these cases, found in the trade press, underscores the fact that the technology revolution in sales is not only coming, but is already well under way.

But revolutions, while often successful, are not always happy. As the first part of the Wilson story shows, with those bored salesmen wasting half the weekend hovering over their computers, sometimes the arrival of automation tools can make jobs worse rather than better. At least the Wilson story has a happy ending. In thousands of other companies across America, the arrival of sales force automation has meant servitude for salespeople, not liberation.

What then can we learn from these cases, and from high

technology itself, that we can use to create a motivated, productive Informed Sales Force instead of a collection of resentful Sales Force Automatons?

History suggests three laws that we can use as a basis for achieving Total Sales Quality and, from it, an Informed Sales Force:

1. *Radical technological change will continue through the rest of your career. If you don't cope with it, you will be left behind.*

Like the Chinese fable of the grains of rice on a chess-board, the power of microprocessors, memory, computing, and telecommunications has at least doubled every 18 months for the last quarter century. And, rather than slow-ing, the rate actually may accelerate. Nowhere is this more the case than with the so-called "computer-on-a-chip," the microprocessor, invented at Intel Corporation in 1970. It was in studying the advancements of this miraculous device that Intel cofounder Dr. Gordon Moore discovered this doubling process, now known as Moore's Law. It states:

The combined factors of processing speed, size, and cost of the latest mi-croprocessor improves by a factor of two every 18 months.

The microprocessor has revolutionized every industry it has touched because by installing intelligence into a prod-uct it suddenly imparts to that product the ability to learn from use, to be improved without having to be physically changed, and to expand into applications that heretofore would have been impossible. It is not surprising then that each new generation of microprocessors creates a host of new markets.

Microprocessors and their supporting chips also work in a synergistic relationship with the larger systems into which they are designed. For example, test and measurement instruments, such as oscilloscopes, have been around for a half century. But the arrival of the microprocessor gave them new life by adding greater precision, adaptability, and programmability. Returning the favor, these upgraded instruments are in turn used to test various features of the next generation of microprocessors.

The most extraordinary example of this virtuous cycle is in computers. Microprocessors may be computers on chips, but their existence makes possible even more powerful new computers . . . which increases the demand for the next generation of microprocessors. Thus, the Intel 8080 of 1975 was as powerful as the building-sized ENIAC of 1945. Its descendant, the 80386 (1985) was equal to the legendary IBM 360 mainframe computers of the 1960s. Two generations later, the Intel Pentium (1993) has stuffed into one square inch all the power of an early 1980s supercomputer.

The Pentium, and its counterpart, the Motorola/IBM/ Apple PowerPC, are marvels of miniaturization. Each contains more than 3,000,000 transistors—switches—which is more than all the transistors there were in the world in 1950. And before they are retired, each of these microprocessors will sell 100 million or more units.[15]

It is the microprocessor's combination of power and pervasiveness that has kicked off the modern information revolution. So the question is: when will it stop? When does the circuitry on the surface of the microprocessor get so small that it runs into the wall of physics, or the chip burns itself up, or the manufacturing processes needed for the miniaturization runs out of gas?

The simple answer is that it probably won't stop. Plan on living and working in a world of perpetual change for the rest of your life. Certainly there are some technical obstacles for the microprocessor out there, but solutions already seem to be in the works. Before then you will likely have on your desk something like a gallium arsenide cube, floating in a shoebox-sized tank of liquid nitrogen . . . and it will have all of the processing power of every computer now in the world.

2. Technology always transforms work.

Since the ENIAC computer was introduced in 1945, computing has grown by 32 orders of magnitude (10^{32}, or 100,000,000,000,000,000,000,000,000,000,000 times) with corresponding improvements in price, size, and performance. Outside of the cosmos itself, almost nothing in human experience can match this rate of change. It only took a two-orders-of-magnitude improvement in power to kick off the Industrial Revolution, four orders to get to the atomic bomb. Yet the Pentium and PowerPC are a thousand times more powerful than the chips Moore was looking at. By the turn of the century, the leading microprocessors will be more than a hundred times as powerful as they are today. And, amazingly enough, we are probably no more than halfway through this period of change. Just looking into the near future we can already visualize three-

The Hurried Pace of Change

dimensional television, computer graphics indistinguishable from real life, instantaneous access to all of the world's knowledge, accurate weather modeling, and soon . . . and even those miracles may pale next to the as-yet-unimaginable things that come after them.

It is this relentless, inexorable advance of microprocessor performance that has overturned every industry, every profession, every corporate office in its path. It cannot help but do so; the new tools are so powerful, confer so much competitive advantage upon their users, that they cannot safely be ignored.

The progress described by Moore's Law can occur in several ways:

• *Pure performance:* Each new advance in processors means that more and more power can be put into existing products. This in turns means the descendants of these products can enter markets that previously were closed or nonexistent. The best example of this is the evolution of applications for the personal computer from spreadsheets to full-motion video and multimedia.

• *Price:* Established processor designs, left unchanged, undergo a rapid price reduction. For example, a typical brand-new microprocessor model may cost $1000 apiece, but five years later it may be available for ten bucks. At this low price, it can now be designed into consumer goods and other highly price-sensitive products. That's the reason for the boom in "smart" appliances and toys.

• *Size:* This also relates to power consumption. The more powerful a microprocessor, the more integrated it usually is. That means it requires fewer and fewer supporting circuits. And that in turn means smaller product dimensions and the portability that comes from using a battery for power instead of the wall plug. Combine that with comparable improvements in semiconductor memory chips and display technology and, in the best-known example, the power of desktop computers is suddenly available in palmtop versions.

Once we understand these three manifestations of Moore's Law, the path of technology's steady march through the corporation becomes more understandable. Accounting and finance were the first to be transformed because their applications were data heavy and required the services of powerful computers. The size of those computers was not critical. Manufacturing applications took a little longer, because here the data were more complex, and the computers often not only gathered and processed information coming in from terminals on the factory floor, but directed machine tools and robots as well.

Research and development was even more complicated. Now you needed very powerful computers capable of performing three-dimensional modeling, storing extensive design libraries, and presenting everything in a graphic format. But helping the cause was the comparatively high budgets of these operations. Had the corporate R&D department needed to wait until engineering workstations cost not $10,000 but $1,000, that technological revolution would be happening only now.

Human resources and customer support functions were next. They took longer because the nature of the data was different. Now instead of financial figures or engineering dimensions, the stuff to be processed was long, complicated personnel records, histories of purchases, etc. The hardware requirements too were more complex: client-server systems combining powerful computers with huge memories to store databases, linked up through very fast communications systems to sophisticated personal computers capable of handling this onrush of data as well as taking on some of the processing activities themselves. These kinds of computers, both large and small, as well as the communications set-up, weren't even available until the late 1980s, and are now only just affordable to small- and medium-sized firms.

And now, finally, sales. Sales has had to wait this long for technology because it requires more sophistication than all of the other applications. A powerful client-server system is only the foundation. Now, the big central server must have access to all of the other departments in the company—not just financial records, but engineering diagrams, parts lists, inventory records, and on and on. Next, the communications grid must be not only hard-wired between offices, but able to reach around the world to distant sales offices . . . and from there go over telephone lines, even wireless radio, to the salespeople in the field.

Once the information gets to the field, it must go to a computer or comparable device that is capable of handling that rate of data, has the ability to take customer input and send it back to the main computer, and, most important, has sufficient processing speed and screen quality to present the data in a compelling and informative way, not only to the salesperson, but to the customer as well.

If all of that isn't enough, there are two more giant hurdles to bringing technology to sales: these computers also have to be small and portable enough to be taken into the field, usually on batteries, and still be inexpensive enough both for the company to purchase in hundreds of units, and for the individual salesperson to buy for personal use.

Thus the sales revolution is occurring now because, despite the enormous advances of the last four decades, only now *can* it occur. Companies such as Oracle and Informix didn't introduce their client-server computer software until the mid-1980s. The telephone system couldn't carry high-speed data communications until the advent of fiber optics and computerized switching systems in the last decade. Wireless is still being developed. True laptop computers didn't arrive until the early 1990s, and only now, thanks to new 3.3-volt "green" ICs, are the new models capable of running for more than a couple of hours on batteries.

The biggest bottleneck, ironically, has been micro-processors. Processor technology may be racing forward at breakneck speed, but that's still not fast enough for our imaginations. Armed with Moore's Law, we know where chips are going and what they will be able to do, and we want to be there *now.* Thus, by the late 1970s we knew that high-level graphics would be possible on personal comput-ers, but we had to wait until the 1990s to get them. Only with the introduction of the Intel 80486 (1989) and the Mo-torola 68040 (1991), both million-plus-transistor micro-processors, was the dream of the mainframe computer-on-a-chip finally realized, making true personal computer graphics practical.

The same forces and delays were at work at the server level as well. The microprocessor had also revolutionized the large computer business, making those monsters smaller, cheaper, and yet more powerful. Moore's Law operated at this level too. To build the kind of high-speed transactional (that is, real-time interacting) "enterprise" servers required for customer service and sales applications, computer designers needed extremely powerful (60+ million transactions per second) microprocessors, such as the MIPS R6000, the Sun SPARCchip and the Digital Equipment Alpha AXP. They weren't available in volume until the beginning of the 1990s.

That is just the hardware. Software capable of taking full advantage of the newest hardware advances takes notoriously long to produce. Writing those thousands of lines of computer code, even using some of the new automation tools, takes time. The influential Apple Macintosh graphical user interface first appeared in 1984, but its counterpart for the more common IBM-compatible personal computers, Microsoft Windows 95, didn't reach the market until 1995. Software for manufacturing automation, first introduced fifteen years ago, is still being perfected.

3. *Technology always presents an apparent dilemma between the control of centralization and the empowerment of decentralization. Choose decentralization every time.*

An enduring myth of modern life is that information technology is on a trajectory to create a better, more liberated world. This utopian notion, promulgated largely by manufacturers, computer freaks, and trade magazines, is at odds with the older fear that automation is inherently controlling and dehumanizing.

The real answer is that it is both. Technological revolutions are two-edged swords, forever placing before us a series of choices between the gathering together of information and its dissemination.

Initially the most appealing choice is always toward centralization and control. That's because, typically, institutions use their new technology to make order out of chaos. Records are disappearing, file cabinets are filled, orders are being lost, no one knows if key parts were ordered—and thus to regain control over operations that have slipped their leash. And technology lends itself beautifully to that task. In fact, the very first computing systems, from the Hollerith punch cards used in nineteenth-century censuses to the construction of ENIAC to compute artillery ballistics, were devised for just this sort of task. Not surprisingly, in almost every business discipline where technology has been put to use, it has initially been used for just this sort of control.

But, as we now know, in the long run this choice of remedy can prove as destructive as the problem it set out to cure. The mainframe computer in the payroll department may solve the problem of keeping employee salary records, but later it becomes the chief obstacle to implementing new flexible pay programs for special employees. The CIM computer running the factory initially increases throughput, but in time makes impossible any competitive mass customization programs. And, relevant to this book, the big new Sales Force Automation system starts out to give the sales force new tools and greater information, but eventually enslaves it.

The second path, towards decentralization, is far more frightening. For one thing, it works against institutional momentum. *After all, we bought these damn computers to organize this mess, now we're going to use them to create a new mess?*

The Hurried Pace of Change

Also, it can threaten the careers of those individuals who manage the centralization of data. But most of all, it threatens management by putting power into the hands of those people out on the line, or in the field, which results in—apparently—a commensurate loss of control by management. And, since traditional management is built upon the acquisition of ever greater control and power, this reversal is not going to be taken lightly by those in charge.

But interestingly, those companies that have empowered their work force, be they giants like Hewlett-Packard or little companies like Ross Valve or Badger Meter, have discovered the central paradox of modern management: *the less control you have the more power you can obtain.*

The parallel is to the technology itself. Hold on to a patent or a new design and you risk losing your market; but license that idea and enlist enough players to make it an industry standard and you may prove wildly successful. So too the manager who tries to keep his or her thumb on the employees may find that those employees have been so hindered in their ability to cope with change that the entire enterprise is at risk. On the other hand, free those employees to make their own decisions quickly, and both the company and the manager's career may thrive.

If we take these three laws—accept the inevitability of technological change, recognize the continuous transformation of work, and choose decentralization over control—then we have a powerful tool for judging which new technologies are appropriate and which, appealing though they may be, are not.

Using this tool to judge each of the Sales Force Automation technologies in turn, we get some real surprises. It

seems that some of the most heralded inventions and products of recent years may actually make the sales process
worse. Below are listed the key sales industries, each with a
comparison between the Sales Force Automation approach
and that of Virtual Selling.

TRAINING

•*Sales Force Automation Approach:* As we have all experienced, most corporate training remains rooted in the
old ways: company policy books and on-the-job training,
usually from company veterans. In the few cases where
SFA even addresses the question of training, it typically
tackles only the former. There are two reasons for this.
First, because most SFA programs are top down and
standardized, they simply don't have the flexibility to deal
with the ever-changing, subjective lessons taught by peers
in the field. But even more important, they *don't want
to.* The whole point of centralization is control, and with
control the last thing you want is older employees
mentoring younger ones in the tricks of the trade—
especially when many of those tricks involve circumvent-
ing corporate controls. On the contrary, what the centralized organization wants, and what SFA reinforces, is a
homogeneity of the sales force around a few established
"policies."

•*Virtual Selling Model:* Educational researchers have long
known that the best training occurs when the pedagogy is
embedded into the work itself. You might call this True
On-the-Job-Training. Instead of weeks of coursework and
lectures, or studying texts and product data sheets at home

at night, the new salesperson actually begins working right away, supported by the information system. In the simplest form, the salesperson has at hand all of the product data, configurations, prices, etc., needed to make the sale. In a more sophisticated version, the salesperson can shorten the learning curve by electronically "visiting" the work of more experienced salespeople to learn the processes and sales steps that have been proven most successful in the past. And, in the most sophisticated Virtual Selling training format, the new salesperson is assisted in these efforts by a *software agent,* "chunks of computer code"[16] that act as intelligent surrogates to help the neophyte search out information as it is needed.

The first of these software agents will be essentially sophisticated electronic search functions. But in time, they will become even more active partners. Predicts *Sales & Marketing Management:*

> Hyper-agents, or avatars, are agents that not only seek out, but act. They'll make appointments, reschedule dates, check out the weather, and answer phone calls. In effect, they will act as [the salesperson's] shadow representative in the electronic world.[17]

Electronic agents and avatars represent both a new generation of software and the death of centralized organization. Those companies that have not already transformed themselves by the time these programs arrive will find them not friendly assistants to their sales force, but electronic gremlins, destroying all attempts at control.

NETWORKS

•*Sales Force Automation Approach:* The traditional network model, one that reinforces centralized control, is a top-down system combining a powerful host server (typically a mainframe computer) that primarily receives raw data from multiple "dumb" terminals. Not surprisingly, with this architecture, almost all power over company information resides at the top . . . hence the rise of "Information Czars" at many corporations. Even with the advent of the modern client-server network, with its use of personal computers and other intelligent client machines, the tendency of most SFA systems is still to keep the flow as unidirectional from the field to headquarters as possible. The result is that while the salesperson in the field may now be armed with a powerful data processing device, this device essentially dumbs down in its interaction with the home office.

•*Virtual Selling Model:* Clearly the traditional model cannot work in an environment in which individual salespeople are given not only autonomy but a central role in decision making. Here the challenge is not to replace the hardware—most of the right equipment is already in place—but to change the mind-set of the people running that hardware. Once again, as with so many things in the new corporation, we have to start looking into the other end of the telescope.

Now the client computers manage the processing, with the servers (at last living up to the name) functioning as the repository of common information or supporting data. One immediate result is that each salesperson begins to construct his or her own work procedures according to what is most efficient—not, as in the past, adjust to the peculiarities of the technology. And where the idea of the mobile, "virtual" office is possible with client-servers and SFA, such a facility becomes a centerpiece of Total Sales Quality. An Informed Sales Force is one that is focused on productivity and success, not upon tools, location, or reports.

DOCUMENT MANAGEMENT

•*Sales Force Automation Approach:* The maintenance of documents in SFA is only marginally improved over the traditional technique, which is to carry around loads of paper brochures, data sheets, specifications, order forms, and so forth, in the trunk of your car. There has even been a whole methodology developed for how to organize automobile trunks for greater productivity. Wrote one trade magazine:

> One way to spend less time fishing in the trunk for brochures and samples is to invest in desk-type organizers such as portable hanging-file cases and storage boxes . . . salespeople who keep their trunks organized spend 38 percent less time looking for papers and samples—a savings of approximately 23 hours per year . . . [18]

Of course, most of this added productivity is lost if, as is usually the case, the brochures are out-of-date, obsolete, or not related to the sale at hand.

Technology, from laptop computers to high-quality portable printers, has overcome many of these problems—and here Sales Force Automation has already made some important contributions. Today, as we saw with the Wilson Sporting Goods example, it is now possible for the salesperson to download extensive product information, inventory data and collateral material such as brochures and data sheets directly from the server computer onto personal computer disks. Once there, the relevant document can be quickly accessed via key words. What's more, the materials can be regularly updated at the home office to keep them from becoming obsolete.

• *Virtual Selling Model:* As important as these SFA achievements are, they only go halfway. As the Wilson example also showed, this regular downloading of masses of information not only burdens the individual salesperson, but the information itself is quickly obsolete. The next step is to make the communication two-way and in real time, so that records are instantly modified to account for each new sale as it occurs.

And that is just the start. An Informed Salesperson is not a passive receptor for the last brochure pumped out of corporate; rather, he or she is an active participant, customizing the material to the unique needs of each potential customer. This means having the ability to modify collateral materials, right down to inserting the customer's name in the text. It also means the ability to cut and paste materials from several different documents, as well as to add fresh copy, in order to construct a new, perhaps one-time-only, document.

While such freedom is technically possible now with most SFA software and hardware systems, it is unlikely without the underlying philosophical shift to Virtual Selling This difference will become acute with the impending arrival of multimedia computing.

Multimedia tools, from laser disks and CD-ROMs to full motion video and 3-D modeling, will transform sales forever. But here too the battle between control and empowerment will assert itself. Will the sales force be supplied with general-purpose, albeit high quality, video presentations? Or will individual salespeople be able to modify those presentations with productions of their own? Will the multimedia presentations be used as point-of-sale systems to take orders from customers, or will the salesperson be able to sit down with the individual customer and explore, interactively, new configurations and designs? The reader can decide which alternative will lead to greater sales productivity.

COMMUNICATIONS

•*Sales Force Automation Approach:* Here too, technology has brought profound changes, and existing SFA software has taken intelligent advantage of those advances.

Unquestionably the greatest historical advance in sales technology was the telephone. The second greatest was the computer, though its effects are still incomplete. Until recently, the two technologies have been separate . . . and the manual labor required to cross the great divide between taking the incoming phone call and accessing the relevant database (not to mention the high number of inaccuracies) has proven to be one of the biggest costs of many volume-based businesses.

Two forces have begun to close this gap. The first, thanks to high speed modems, fiber optics, and other new technologies, is that data processing and telecommunications are beginning to merge. By the turn of the century, the personal computer, telephone, phone recorder, fax, modem, copier, and laser printer will all be essentially in the same box.

One immediate effect upon sales of this merger is an improvement in the productivity and quality of telephone sales. Incoming calls can now be automatically recognized and properly routed to the proper individual or information source.

Field sales will also feel the effect in several ways. As with the Vulcan Binding & Cover example, labor costs saved in telephone sales can be shifted to the field. So too can field salespeople be freed to focus on larger accounts. Moreover, customers, walked through the phone-mail gauntlet of questions, become self-qualifying, their call and accompanying records automatically routed to the right salesperson. But perhaps most importantly, the same computer/telecommunications equipment also gives the field quicker and more accurate access to the corporate information files it needs to stay updated with customers.

The second technological force is the rise of wireless telecommunications. With wireless, the salesperson in the field can at last have the level of access that was until now only possible from a telephone, or, better, from a desktop computer hooked up to a modem. Wireless means instant access from wherever the salesperson is, transmitting new orders and downloading updated records and sales materials.

The Hurried Pace of Change

• *Virtual Selling Model:* Once again, as it is currently designed, Sales Force Automation, trapped by its own inner dynamic, can only take the communications revolution in sales half way.

The real revolution in communications is not in speed and access, impressive as those gains are, but in *interactivity.* The combining of voice and data allows the rapid two-way transfer of massive amounts of multimedia information in real time. Qualifying and routing customers is one thing. But imagine a salesperson, sitting in a customer's parking lot just before going in, calling up on a laptop computer the record of every contact made with this customer in the last two weeks, every order that this customer has made in the last year, and personal background material on the individual being contacted today.

That's just the start. How about if the salesperson can now check his or her phone messages and, at the same time, print out a new custom brochure that incorporates the client's name and business? That done, what if the salesperson can then call up, by two-way video on the computer screen, a contact at the factory to find out if production of a critical component is still tracking on schedule? Then perhaps a second video call to service and support to find out if the customer's complaint last week was properly handled—followed by a print-out of all communications made between those two parties since then?

That's the kind of empowerment the new communications/computing technologies make possible. How many centralized organizations would dare put this much power into the hands of their sales force?

WORK TEAMS

•*Sales Force Automation Approach:* Traditional sales teams are usually highly structured, last longer than they are effective, and are imposed from above. Typically such teams are created to tackle a large prospective customer or to maintain an existing one.

Philosophically, Sales Force Automation supports this older model through its structured approach to "groupware." The formation of teams still requires management approval, the modification of programs to allow lateral linkages, and the swapping of file security codes (and sometimes not even that). The result is a sales environment that intrinsically works against the formation of true teams, against the sharing of information, and worst of all, against working together for the greater good of the company.

•*Virtual Selling Model:* A clue to how this model diverges from the SFA approach can be found in the Vulcan Binding & Cover model. As Vulcan found, productivity—and profits—jumped as salespeople began to share their knowledge. What's more, the salespeople themselves began to appreciate the advantages of teamwork.

Once again, Virtual Selling succeeds by turning the tables on the Sales Force Automation paradigm. Instead of impeding teamwork, Virtual Selling puts it at the heart of the program. And, where the traditional model enforces calcified, often internally suspicious teams, this model is organized for spontaneous, cross-disciplinary *ad hoc* teams that may last for just minutes or may endure for years—their longevity defined solely by need.

How is this done? By combining improved communications with empowered individuals. Informed Salespeople need to be able to bounce effortlessly through the organization, gathering information or talking to individuals as needed, without worrying about rigid hierarchical organization structures, inaccessible data bases, or secret files. Certainly each employee needs a private electronic work area, but beyond that, *everything should be accessible to everyone.* And once that is achieved, the creation of fluid teams inevitably follows.

Does all of this accessibility raise concerns about security? Absolutely, but not as great concerns as one might imagine. Many companies are fearful about security because they are built on distrust of their employees—and the employees understandably respond in kind. And here, once again, Virtual Selling as part of the larger trend towards "learning," "agile," "virtual" corporations, turns the tables. At the heart of employee empowerment is trust. Trust is also the foundation of Virtual Selling. Thus, to succeed, the company must learn to trust its sales force . . . and the resulting Informed Sales Force will return that trust in spades.

Now, let's go back to the prosaic little MO-V, the mobile office in a van, and why it is symbolic.

We have seen in this chapter that rapid technological change will be with us for many years to come. And indeed, we can think of the MO-V as being Moore's Law made manifest. Just twenty years ago the sight of such a rig would have struck the average salesperson dumb. Now, a more typical answer might be: "Well, it's about time"—underscoring the fact that, although we may be resistant to technological change, we are nevertheless assimilating it at an enormous rate.

But the MO-V represents more than that. It succeeds because it is an *appropriate* use of technology. It accomplishes exactly what it set out to do: give a salesperson a place to work while, literally, on the road. It liberates the sales professional from the confines of his office, makes him productive during what were once lost hours—and at the same times empowers him by giving him the technology he needs to do his job. In the battle between centralization/control and decentralization/empowerment, the MO-V people made the right choices . . . which is more than can be said for the billion-dollar companies that implemented CIM or are installing SFA programs right now. In the end, success always comes to those who place human needs over the demands of technology.

There is one more lesson we can derive from our little van, one so obvious (or perhaps so transparent) that the original magazine story never mentions it. Among all the glittering electronics products associated with the MO-V, the greatest may well be the one nobody notices: the Chevy van itself. Very likely it contains, in its motor, dashboard, transmission, and electrical system, more microprocessors and other integrated circuits than all of the office equipment combined. We forget that fact because *the most appropriate technology becomes invisible.*

This is the acid test for any new technology, be it personal digital assistants (PDAs) like the Apple Newton, Skypagers, fax-modem boards for computers, or all those inventions still on the drawing boards. All of the hype, all of the performance specifications, attached to these inventions are meaningless. The only thing that really counts is the potential for continuous improvement towards ever-greater productivity. When it works right a new invention seamlessly enters our professional or personal lives; when it doesn't, it remains a novelty or becomes an irritant. Either way, it remains unused.

The rotary phone, the digital phone, and now the cellular phone have all become invisible to the sales professional. So have the airplane, the copier, the fax machine and the desktop computer. So too has e-mail and phone mail. But, as the surveys show, much of what we have called Sales Force Automation, both hardware and software, has not become invisible—and, because it is "inappropriate," it never will.

As we now start down the alternative path to the Informed Sales Force, it is crucial that we not make the same mistake. Propelling us forward is Moore's Law, which will soon put the power of the modern supercomputer, ten million transistors, on a single silicon chip. This will in turn present a cornucopia of thrilling new applications, from full-motion video demonstrations to animated point-of-sale tools to the modeling of mass customized products right at the customer's desk. The call will again be to throw this technology at sales, then to demand that it be used and for its control to remain in the hands of management. And that will again be the makings of a disaster.

Instead, we must stick to what is human and what is appropriate to real-life selling. That is, we need to understand every nuance of the sales process to see the pressure points where technology can, invisibly, be inserted to improve the productivity and morale of real salespeople. We already know the technology will be there—for example, within the decade, everything contained in the MO-V van will be held in a device in the palm of your hand. The real challenge is to meet it with the right applications.

And that leads to a great irony. Virtual Selling, at first glance, may seem a tool to bring new technologies to the sales process—but in fact, it is a filter, dipped into the flood of new inventions to allow only those that are appropriate to pass into use. And, though the Total Sales Quality is ostensibly our goal, the very zenith of Virtual Selling—in fact, if we do our job right and the technology we employ really becomes invisible, then as we approach Total Sales Quality it too will become invisible—and the Informed Sales Force, though resting on powerful technology, will be the most humane of organizations.

Chapter 5

Virtual *Reality*

Thus far we have been racing forward toward a new technology-driven but people-empowering model for sales. Now, for this chapter, we need to stop for a moment, catch our breath, and look at some harsh realities.[1]

We'll provide here a specific outline of what you should be looking for in selecting a sales force automation solution. Let's explore exactly how to put together a system that will allow your organization to realize the benefit of Virtual Selling.

We'll discuss some trends that we see in computing, specifically, software—trends that we see in client/server computing and what impact they will have on the sales force automation market. Now, what we are doing here is a very risk-fraught venture but we are going to try to look into our crystal ball and evaluate the impact of these technologies upon the sales force automation software problem in the second half of this decade.

Virtual Selling

The essential sales automation problem focuses upon the deployment of a high-end system with the requisite functionality to serve your purposes going forward including comprehensive customer information systems, product information systems, competitive information systems, and decision support systems, deployed multinationally, multilingually in multiple currencies—comprehensive closed-loop sales and marketing information systems.

Clearly, there's a lot of interest in this space. At this time, this is the fastest growing segment of the client/server application software market. This is a $750 million software market growing at a 48 percent compound annual growth rate. Putting this into perspective, this is the same absolute growth that the relational data-base market experienced from 1986 to 1991. This is becoming a huge market segment that is growing very rapidly.

As we consider hardware and software technologies that are applicable to solve the software automation problem, there's a number of things we need to address. The first is software product architecture. We want to look for architectures that are complete and robust. The product architecture is going to do much more than simply provide the functionality, the user interface, and the platform support; it is going to determine whether a product is going to endure, whether you're going to be replacing it in two or three years, whether it will scale to large sets of users, and whether it will allow you to continue to exploit emerging technologies that are coming on-line in the second half of this decade.

Whether you are building a Virtual Selling system or buying one, the essential operational constraints that you are going to have to face in the Sales Force Automation space are that the solution be functionally complete, support multitiered distribution strategies, provide high levels of configurability, and, finally, scale to meet the needs of even the largest organizations.

By functionally complete, we mean one fully integrated application solution with one common user interface. We mean an integrated opportunity management system, sales management system, product configurator, marketing encyclopedia, customer information system, market information system, and competitive information system. Historically one of the problems with sales force automation systems is that they have been functionally trivial. We look at things like contact managers or product configurators or product forecasters or order entry systems that have been called sales force automation systems, and we think they are not. They are merely partial point solutions that solve maybe one-twentieth of the problem. Comprehensiveness is a primary operational constraint.

Secondly, any such systems are going to have to offer complete support for multitiered distribution strategies.

In the seventies and the eighties, companies used resellers, field sales, retail outlets, or VARs for their distribution channel. In the second half of this decade, this is just not the case. Large-scale organizations are deploying multitiered distribution strategies including a combination of telesales, telemarketing, direct marketing, resellers, VARs, and field sales.

Any sales information system that you deploy has got to offer complete support for multitiered distribution strategies. This has to go forward into agentless sales as we move into the internet and interactive television. Why is it important to think about these things? These investments are not 12- or 24-month investments. Largely, the investments we make in the structure of these information systems will determine what we can do in our markets, how we can compete, and how we will be constrained by our information systems.

A sales information system has to offer total configurability. When we install the system, it needs to fit like a glove and look like the business that we're operating or the business that we want to operate. It should not require us to change our business operations to meet the constraints of some software-hardware system. There are some real exciting technologies that have come on-line in the last couple of years that we can apply to this configuration problem. With some of these object-oriented application development technologies like C++ and OLE 2 compliant business objects, we can provide levels of configurability at the object code level that we could never do before. Your sales application needs to support large-scale UNIX and Windows NT servers, workstations in call centers, nomadic laptops, small form factor computers, and wireless PDA devices.

Microsoft has provided a real service to the world as it relates to the client side of this equation in 1995 and beyond. When we put together the product standards in the client-server market in the early eighties, we talked to large-scale MIS organizations, and they had no idea whether they would be computing on 3270 devices running against IBM mainframes, on HP, DEC, DG, Stratus, Harris, or Apollo equipment, or on CPM machines that were coming out of Digital Research. Many software companies implemented a strategy to develop "portable" software that could be run on a wide range of computing environments.

This was a very successful strategy in the last decade. A lot of other companies emulated this strategy and said, "Don't worry—we can run on anything that you'll use." Microsoft has provided a real service to the world in that there is very little argument today on what your company is going to compute on for the client side. You are going to compute on Windows PCs. The game is over—Microsoft has won, and the world is a lot simpler place. Going forward, your application software needs to support Windows clients—fully exploiting the power of OLE 2, Microsoft Office compatibility, MAPI messaging integration, 32-bit processing capacity, and Windows 95 user interface standards.

Sales information systems clearly have got to run on industry standard relational data-base servers. The nice thing about companies like Oracle, Sybase, and Informix is they offer complete support for the different client-server computing environments.

Object-oriented technology is going to be very important. We will need to be able to employ very highly distributed applications taking advantage of what we call replication server technology that's now being delivered by companies like Microsoft, Informix, Oracle, and Sybase. The replication server technology allows us to have these servers and data stores replicated around the world.

If we want to automate a General Motors, a Sony, a Unilever, or a Procter & Gamble, we will need replication servers distributed around the globe to handle both the data distribution issues and the concurrency issues. Replication services are very important.

When you look at the state of the art today for configuring large manufacturing or financial applications, you see companies like SAP or Oracle that deliver a version of the source code to the customer's site. Then, a small army of consultants from one of your favorite consulting companies modifies that source code and the underlying data entities and relationships. They go into SAP R3 or SQL*Forms source code and modify the application logic to meet the needs of the business, and then they leave a customized version of the source code at the customer's site.

Well, the process is long, arduous, and expensive. It makes it very difficult to support the customer and, most important, how do you install Version 2? How do you rev the software without having to fold all of the source-code changes back into it? This is incredibly expensive.

Modern application software is fully object oriented. Configurable business objects are the key to rapidly deployed, highly customized applications. This is a primary operational constraint.

As we move into the second half of this decade, there's a lot of exciting things going on. There are video phones, full-motion video, wireless, 32-bit processing, new human interface technology, and software agent technology. Software providers are going to be building support for these new technologies into new versions of their products. Unless you have a product built with a modern, robust product architecture, you will not be able to exploit the utility of these new technologies.

There are a couple of messages here. The first is that in the last few years a lot of real exciting technology has come on-line. We want to make sure that we exploit these developments, and more importantly, that we are in a position to exploit what's happening in the next few years. We think that a technology solution today needs to support both Windows 3.1 and 16-bit processing and be able to run seamlessly on Windows 95 and Windows NT as a 32-bit application. We think that, as it relates to office systems, products have to work with Microsoft Office. We need to support both UNIX servers today and Windows NT servers tomorrow. We need support for not only client/server today, but also we need to address the problems associated with the data synchronization of intermittently connected client machines. Going forward, it is very clear that wireless support will become important. We need an environment that allows us to rapidly configure business requirements of the user organization.

Whatever solution you deploy needs to be enabled for global markets. Your company is either in the global marketing business or gearing up for global markets . . . or going out of business. The application needs to be fully globalized. What does this mean? It means multiple currency and national language support. It means double-byte character support. The application needs to look like a Chinese application in China and a German application in Germany and be able to roll up into whatever the common currency you use to run the business globally.

Your software architecture needs to scale to meet the needs of the large growing multinational organizations, running against fully distributed relational data bases supporting replication and synchronization. A lot of these requirements are covered just by supporting Informix, Oracle, Sybase, or Microsoft SQL Server.

Your Virtual Selling solution needs to scale to thousands of users with complete support for three-tiered computing architectures. This is where we have Windows clients, UNIX servers, and IBM mainframe back-ends in large organizations. We need intelligent communications capability to handle the software problems associated with intermittently connected users. There are users who are traveling, doing remote work for a few days, updating their forecasts, putting notes in systems, requesting approvals on quotes, wanting to send letters to customers, adding notes to the customer history file and then reconnecting from a motel room or the office, sending the deferred request to the server side, and re-synchronizing with client side with new leads, product information, and competitive information.

Any solution an organization is deploying for use in the second half of this decade has to have an application programmatic interface (API) to support an enterprise-wide computing model. The solution must be able to seamlessly integrate with the mainstream financial and manufacturing applications that are being delivered today by companies like Dun & Bradstreet, Oracle, and SAP. We need to be integrated with the inventory control, order entry, accounts receivable, and commission systems. The virtual sales system needs to be an integral component of an enterprise-wide computing model, not just a stand-alone lead tracking system.

Tight integration with ACDs and PBXs is critical. Perhaps, more importantly though in the next few years, video conferencing is going to become an increasingly key component of business-to-business commerce. As we're talking to our customer on the phone, they will be looking at us on their video phone. While they are doing that, why not click a mouse and do a product demonstration at 30 frames a second?

Virtual *Reality*

The compression and transmission technology is in place. All you need is the video phone to do a customer testimonial at 30 frames a second or page through your product proposal on your customer's video phone. When you think about your architecture today, this is difficult to do. We suggest it will not be difficult to do in 1996 given the proper product architecture. All you need is the video phone. We think our friends in the telecom companies are going to make that a very affordable ubiquitous device.

You need an architecture that will support electronic documents. You can do this today with technologies coming from a number of companies. There are on-line marketing encyclopedias supporting full text search of all the thousands of color brochures, annual reports, and data sheets that we use. Print them. Put them on your customer's video phone. Fax them to the customer while you are talking to him. Show them to the customer while visiting customers.

This information needs to be immediately accessible to the sales professional. You need to support more rich data types including audio and full motion video for product demonstrations and customer testimonials. It is clearly possible today to build architectures that will support these. The technologies that have come on-line in the last couple years, including C++, MFC, OLE 2, client/server, 32-bit processing, and new user interface associated with Windows 95, allow you to do things at levels of functionality and scalability that were previously impossible.

We can now solve problems like delivering a system that is functionally complete, that will scale to meet the needs of large users, that can be very rapidly modified to meet the needs of the organizations where the installation is taking place, and that is based on a modern technology foundation. It's important to exploit the next wave of technology to establish the potential for long-term strategic competitive advantage. We have this big step function of technology that's now available to you to build these applications. Use it.

Let's look forward a few years at the next step function in technology. Be in a position to use small form factor computing and wireless multimedia. Software agent technology is going to be very important in this application class. Essentially software agents are chunks of computer code with high levels of intelligence. We can have a software agent recommend the next step in a sales cycle. A software agent evaluating the semantics of the information associated with an opportunity can suggest that if you're selling a particular product in a particular market that a specific competitor may emerge. Picture a salesperson forecasting a $250,000 opportunity with a 90 percent probability of closure this month and—oh, by the way—he hasn't given that customer a proposal yet; we don't need a sales manager to tell the salesperson that his forecast needs to be adjusted. A software agent can do that very readily.

In the second half of this decade, the whole design philosophy for systems, and not only sales automation systems, is going to change. These systems used to be about control. With the old Sales Force Automation systems, managers got real excited back at headquarters because they thought they were going to know everything that's going on in their world. They'd be just like a puppet master controlling all of those little puppets. They could look very readily into anybody's activities and see how many sales calls were made last week. What's the status of this particular account? How come that forecast slipped again? Well, as we have found out trying to deploy a number of these systems around the world, they tend to be very short-lived sales automation projects because the salespeople have realized they will outlive the MIS organization in the inevitable political battle that ensues.

Going forward, successful virtual sales systems will have the information flow going down from the corporation to the salespeople. They will be about empowering salespeople to do their jobs—about providing them with the product information, competitive information, market information, and customer information they need to do their jobs.

Now you all know people who are really good salespeople. Perhaps you've met them when buying a car, a house, some software, or a computer. And what are the characteristics of these salespeople? They know their markets. They know the history of their technology. They know their product features and functions. They can explain the difference between the products in their product line. They can compare their product line to the product line of their competitors. They can pick up an article from *Business Week, Road & Track,* or *ComputerWorld* and verify the things that they are saying. They can tell you how much a product costs. They can configure a tailored solution for you. They can tell you when they can deliver it. They can do it on time.

Well, when you find people like that, you buy the house from them. You buy the car from them because they respect your time. They develop an understanding of what it is you're trying to accomplish, and they solve it for you.

They know the history of use within your organization, your family, or your business. They know the three other efforts, three last cars, two last houses, or the other computer systems that you purchased. They know whether these have been successful or unsuccessful. When you find people like that, you do business with them. You follow them from company to company. You hire them and promote them. These are highly informed salespeople.

Now, look at what is going on here. The products that we sell today are getting more and more complex—all products. For example, how many microprocessors are there in an automobile? Hundreds. It's hard to know what all of these products do. Well, we can apply information technologies now. We can put the information very readily at a sales professional's fingertips—a couple of clicks of a mouse or taps of a pen. The sales reps can now deliver the information required to solve the customers' problems.

The information needs to flow downward from corporate to the sales people, creating highly empowered salespeople. It's providing them with the tools that they need to excel at their jobs. It's all carrot and very little stick, and we think that's what the philosophy of these systems going forward will be about.

There's been a lot of talk about Sales Force Automation in the last ten years. It's always been the year of the Sales Force Automation. It's just never quite happened. We can remember when it was that way for the relational data-base market, when there was a lot of talk but it just never quite happened. Then about 1986, the relational data-base market exploded.

When we got into local area networking, it was

always'going to be the year of the LAN. Then in about 1988 or '89, it finally happened. There was all this talk about multimedia but nothing happened in the eighties. Then in the nineties, it exploded. We foresee that this is about to happen now in sales information systems.

There have been a lot of talk about and a lot of people thinking about this market since maybe 1985 or '86, but the market never really happened. Most projects have never really been successful. We suggest that one of the reasons for this is that the underlying technologies were just not there to do the job. The user interface, computing, communications, and rich data-type technologies, and the computing power were not there. The communication bandwidth was not available. No matter how much you tried, if you attempted to deploy a functionally rich sales automation system given the software technologies that were in place in 1986 or even as recently as 1990, it would be a frustrating experience.

As entertaining and exciting as it is to speculate about the bright technological future, the truth is that organizations must forever live in the present. And, while it is easy to guess that the computer of the future will be more powerful than today's supercomputers, yet fit in the palm of your hand, such a prediction tells you next to nothing about what you need to do today to get ready for such a machine.

In fact, as many companies have ruefully discovered, Moore's Law tantalizingly tells you a lot about where we're going, but little about how to get there. Fifteen years ago more than one progressive company bought Wang minicomputers, at that time the hottest models on the market, on the assumption that they were technologically leapfrogging the competition . . . only to end up with obsolete iron from a bankrupt company.

So, how then do you position yourself *now* for a predictable, but undefinable, future? And, assuming you adopt the model of Virtual Selling with its goal of Total Sales Quality, what should you be doing today? How do you begin?

The short answer is that while we cannot discern in detail what the future will bring, Moore's Law does at least suggest both a direction and a set of potentialities. We do know, with some certitude, what the performance of microprocessors—and hence, computers and office products—will be a decade or two from now. We also know from the past that this performance will likely be fully exploited by numerous vendors, and that competition among those firms will quickly drive the price of that performance down into the price range of the average consumer.

We also know something else: unlike Sales Force Automation, with the Total Sales Quality model we have a specific target for what we want. As we've seen, Virtual Selling by an Informed Sales Force has some very distinctive characteristics, including:

- extremely high rates in converting qualified leads to sales
- customer participation in product configuration and design
- increased sales force control over manufacturing
- in-field preparation of sales presentation tools, collateral materials, manuals, and contracts
- company-wide sharing of rich and complex information regarding sales contacts, marketing programs, product inventories, etc.

Armed with this knowledge, it becomes apparent that the target we should be working toward lies at the intersection of Moore's Law and Total Sales Quality. Thus, everything we do now directed toward that point will probably be beneficial over time to the company and increase its likelihood of long-term success . . . while any investment we make, or institutional shift we undertake, that diverges from this path, is likely to be counterproductive and self-destructive.

How far away is that point of intersection where Virtual Selling becomes a practical reality? Closer than you might think. Already, in a world of gigabyte memory banks, client-server information systems and Pentium-based personal computers, perhaps half of all the features of a Virtual Selling program are already possible. New software applications designed to take full advantage of this current hardware will probably get that competence up to two-thirds of the complete model.

That will take until about 1997. By then, the next generation of microprocessors—the Intel P7 and the third generation PowerPCs, as well as competitive offerings from DEC, MIPS, and various clone-makers—will be available in volume. These chips, and the new generations of large computer networks, PCs, and hand-held "personal digital assistants" (PDAs) that they will fill, will be the real hardware of the Total Sales Quality movement. Add two more years for the software tools to catch up—and by the year 2000 every component of the TSQ revolution should be in place. In other words, Virtual Selling, Total Sales Quality, and the creation of an Informed Sales Force should already be in your five-year plan.

Needless to say, in the scope of business planning, century's end is as near as tomorrow. Most big manufacturing companies are already well along in planning new factories and ordering capital equipment for that year. This suggests that, unless they are very, very lucky, most of those companies are already off-track and making huge investments in the wrong business model. They are the CIM-like disasters of the early years of the twenty-first century—taking massive and devastating write-offs, wrecking employee morale and the market's trust, and losing giant chunks of market share to younger (or, ironically, to slower-moving older) competitors. And since, as noted earlier, sales is unique in affecting both sides of the balance sheet, these progressive but misguided companies will suffer a double whammy.

And it will be a very big whammy. The average large company in the United States is expected to make a $10-million to $15-million investment—$15,000 per salesperson—in sales automation systems over the next few years. So the first question you must ask as you plan to automate your sales force is this: Is your firm one of these victims-in-waiting?

HARDWARE

With one eye on this near-future scenario, we can backtrack to the present. Now, for the first time, we can gain a sense of what we should be looking for today in hardware and software, as well as in corporate re-engineering, to start ourselves down the right track.

Let's look first at hardware and operating systems.

In the early 1980s, when companies were first constructing their management information systems, they faced a real dilemma. There were so many possible minicomputer and mainframe platforms to choose from—IBM, DEC, Data General, Stratus, Harris, and Apollo, among others—most with their own proprietary operating systems. Then, confusing things even further, came the arrival of the first desktop computers using the CP/M operating software. The result, as many of us remember, is that customers spent a lot of time and money either trying to jury-rig their computers to keep them functional, or simply junking them for another model.

Luckily for us, the great industry shake-out is now largely over. And the winner is Microsoft Windows, running on the Intel 80x86 series microprocessor architecture. The current version of the former is the Windows 95 operating system; the latest form of the latter is the Intel Pentium.

This is not an opinion but a statement of fact. Thus, while there are thousands of UNIX-based computers in use throughout the world, UNIX as an operating system for PCs has missed its chance to become the universal industry standard. The simple truth is that the Intel/Microsoft standard currently owns 80 percent of the microprocessor/personal computer industry. So, if you are going to make a high-risk bet on the future, your best chance is to go with the leader.

Committing yourself to the Intel/Microsoft standard is hardly a straitjacket these days. In processors alone it is now possible to buy 80x86 versions from not only Intel, but also from Advanced Micro Devices, Cyrix, and Nexgen—and, as the PowerPC, from Motorola and IBM. Furthermore, there are literally hundreds of different vendors offering 80x86-based palmtop, notebook, and desktop computers, from budget clone companies in the Far East to blue-chip manufacturers such as Hewlett-Packard, Compaq, and Dell. Only with the operating system does one company, Microsoft, maintain hegemony . . . though, if history is any indication, that too will someday change.

Given this foundation, we can establish a relatively precise scenario for the equipment that will be used by individual salespeople and their sales offices. It will be notebooks and laptops, and perhaps some powerful PDAs, used by salespeople when they are in the field. These devices will have color screens (for presentations), large memory storage (say 1.5 gigabytes for multimedia customer files, contracts, etc.), high-speed 28.8 kbps internal modems (for talking to the home office), and wireless models. They will be able to operate on 16-bit processors and Windows 3.1 today, while being able to move up smoothly to 32-bit Windows 95 and Windows NT in the next few years. Some of the functions already listed, as well as others specific to the task at hand, will be added to the computer as needed via PCMCIA cards. The salesperson will also be equipped with a second portable device box containing a fax/copier/scanner/laser printer.

This field equipment also suggests the equipment at the sales office that will support this salesperson. Here we see a few desktop computers into which the salesperson can download files for more complex processing and a server-hub that acts as the interface between the salespeople and the home office. For hard-copy presentations, proposals, and manuals, there will also be a color laser printer and a high-speed color copier with binder. And there will be video telephones, frequently windowed on the screens of the office PCs.

So far, pretty straightforward, but now it starts to get tricky. At the corporate level, the situation is less defined. One thing is obvious: the type of enterprise servers needed to create and maintain an Informed Sales Force will be larger and more sophisticated than anything we have in general use today. We already know how to support Virtual Selling by a ten-user telesales department or a ten-user sales organization—and there are a lot of systems on the market today that can easily do that. The problem not yet fully solved is how to support virtual sales in an organization with hundreds, or even thousands, of users—and multiple hundred-gigabyte or even terabyte data stores. Making the situation even more complicated is the likely scenario that in such an organization, perhaps only a few hundred of those users will be fully connected, while thousands of others will be intermittently connected—with the host of data synchronization problems that will likely ensue. Now, add to this chaos the fact that many of those users will themselves have near gigabyte stores on their own computers—information that will largely have to be accessible to the rest of the organization—and you have the makings of a real Gordian knot in IS.

Yet, clearly there are standards emerging here that you can rely upon. Moore's Law keeps relentlessly chugging forward; so the smart money says that a solution will be found. What will that solution look like? Most likely it will be constructed around large-scale UNIX servers. But Windows NT servers, with typical Microsoft single-mindedness when it comes to attacking a market, are also coming on strong. It is unlikely that this competition will be resolved by the end of the decade.

So we have a dilemma: how should you commit yourself to corporate servers? The good news is that you don't have to yet; the solutions you'll need are not yet on the scene, so that buys you a little time. Secondly, because the shake-out may take years to occur, you are probably safe with either operating system. Finally, and most important, this is one area where the data-base software equipment vendors—Oracle, Sybase, Informix—are going to resolve most of these problems for you. Your job is instead to keep an eye on those companies, look past their hype, and be ready when the equipment you need finally arrives on the scene.

What features will you look for in such a server? One is that it will be a true client-server system, capable of seamlessly storing and transferring billions of bytes of multimedia data up and down the organization. This also suggests that it be capable of managing large and geographically diverse relational data bases. Further, it must be fully functional in object-oriented technology in order to speed the creation of new applications. Finally, especially in large organizations, it must support replication server technology—that is, it must be capable of duplicating data and then automatically distributing that data to multiple "replication" servers located throughout the world.

SOFTWARE

Now let's turn to software.

• *Scalability:* The critical term in appraising software for the Informed Sales Force is scalability. In other words, any sales automation tools you buy now must be capable of growing upward in power and sophistication from the individual salesperson to the sales office to a global enterprise network—while never sacrificing the immediate needs of Virtual Selling or the long-term performance goal of Total Sales Quality.

Not an easy task. In fact, probably no more than 1 percent of the popular SFA programs now on the market would qualify under these criteria. Yet, any application or tool short of that standard is essentially a wasted investment.

What qualifies as true enterprise-wide scalability when it comes to sales? Some clues can be found in the preceding section on hardware. So, for example, scalability should include the capability to run against fully distributed relational data bases supporting replication and synchronization. One obvious way to do that is for the software to support Informix, Oracle, Sybase, or Microsoft SQL servers.

That's just the beginning. Your new software should also offer complete support for organizations with what might be called "three-tier" computing architectures—typically large organizations where you find Windows clients, UNIX servers, and IBM mainframe hubs.

Scalability is only the most important of the characteristics that you should be looking for now in purchasing sales automation software. Here are some other things to insist on:

• *Docking Management:* Vitally important is docking management, an intelligent communications capability to handle the challenge of intermittently connected users. In particular, the sales system must be able to deal with users who disconnect from the network, go off for a few days to work on their own computers, then return with such finished items as updated forecasts, notes, requests for approval on quotes, letters that need to be sent to customers, and updated customer history files . . . and want to be able to send all that deferred material in from their office or motel room. Fielding and filing this information and deferred requests will be hard enough, but this management system will also have the task of resynchronizing that client machine with new leads, product information, and competitive data that have arisen since the last contact.

• *Enterprise-wide Computing Support:* To succeed, any sales information system you put in place cannot be just a stand-alone lead tracking system. Rather, it must support an enterprise-wide computing model. In other words, it must be able to integrate seamlessly with the new financial and manufacturing applications being delivered today by companies such as Dun & Bradstreet and Standard & Poors. By the same token, an effective sales system also needs to be integrated with the inventory control, order entry, accounts receivable, and commission systems.

• *Telephony Integration:* In the emerging multimedia corporate environment, telecommunications becomes vitally important. Therefore a good sales system, at the very minimum, will need to be integrated with both automatic call-dialing systems (ACDs) and PBXs.

Long term, the critical factor will be support of video telephony. The video phone and the teleconference will be key components of business-to-business commerce. And, if you are talking face to face with a customer on a video phone, the obvious next step is to click a mouse and conduct a product demonstration or page through a product proposal at 30 frames per second on the video screen. We already have the requisite video compression and transmission technology today; all we need are the video phones. And you can be sure that the telecom companies know this and are soon going to be making those products available at an affordable price. Smart companies will be ready for them.

• *New Media Support:* Documents, in all forms, are the centerpiece of an Informed Sales Force. We need a software architecture that can do three things.

1. It can *already* support text and graphics in the form of letters, quotes, and proposals.
2. It can *now* begin to handle such electronic documentation as literature on-line, conduct full-text searches, and gain quick access to reusable information.
3. It is prepared to *soon* manage such audio- and full-motion-video "document" needs as live product demonstrations, customer testimonials, video news releases and multimedia catalog browsing.

The informed sales professional must be able to search through on-line marketing encyclopedias supporting full text, image, and, eventually, video search through thousands of color brochures, annual reports, data sheets, training videos, speeches, etc.—then print or record them and put them on the customer's video phone or computer screen in real time.

• *Emerging Technologies:* We have discussed some of these in the hardware section, but it doesn't hurt to be reminded that it isn't enough merely to buy the boxes; you also need to support with software the unique features of your new hardware. Wireless telecommunications, personal digital associates (PDAs), pen-based computing, and PCM-CIA have all been mentioned, and all must be accounted for.

There are other technologies as well—such as speech recognition, cable television, video data bases and servers, neural networks, and even home/office controllers—that may play a role someday and should at least be considered.

Finally, there are some new and emerging software categories. The most obvious is multimedia, but there is also the *software agent*. Only in its rudimentary stages as a kind of expert-systems software, the software agent has the potential to become the single most important support function in sales by the beginning of the next century. Already, simple software agent programs can track a customer and suggest the next step to the salesperson. One can easily imagine in a few years agent programs that evaluate the information associated with a particular sales opportunity, then construct for the salesperson not only a sales strategy and point of sale tools, but also a list of likeliest product configurations, price lists, and profiles of potential competitors.

It is interesting to note that when we spoke of hardware, we predicted the future based upon what we already *have*. But in predicting software, the discussion was based upon what we *want*. This says something very important about the amount of control we have over our destiny in each field.

In hardware, controlled as it is by a few key manufacturers, we individual customers have little leverage. About all we can do is jump on board the likely leader. But in software (except Microsoft's hegemony in operating systems), where there are thousands of competitors, each scrambling for a tiny fraction of the market, we do have a voice. And that is all the more reason to understand *now* what we need and then begin demanding it.

ORGANIZATION

If the last thirty years have taught anything in high technology it is that you can make all the right choices in hardware and software and still fail because your company is unprepared to deal with the organizational transformations demanded by those new systems. It will be no different with the automation of sales. In fact, one can say with certainty not only that an Informed Sales Force will only be possible with a new form of corporate organization, but that an ISF, once achieved, will reinforce that new model indefinitely.

There has been no shortage of books and articles about this new organization model, whether it is called agile, fast, flat, or the all-encompassing term *virtual corporation*. So too has a mechanism—*re-engineering*—been codified for getting there. It is beyond the scope of this chapter to go into detail about the virtual corporation, but its rapid acceptance throughout the industrialized world suggests that this is the most likely corporate model for the decades to come and the one to which your company will soon subscribe (if it hasn't already). Therefore, it is important to understand some of the salient features of this model.

1. Virtual corporations are flatter than traditional models. The rapid cycle times under which these firms operate have no time to allow information to filter up slowly through layers of middle management so that a decision can be made by a senior executive. Instead, individuals on the line—salespeople, marketers, factory workers, etc.—are empowered to make their own decisions, middle management largely disappears (or takes on the new task of creating tools), and senior management pulls away from day-to-day decision making to focus on long-term strategy.

2. Hand in hand with employee empowerment goes continuous training of those employees to give them both the technical and interpersonal skills to take responsibility and make informed decisions.

3. Virtual organizations are highly dependent upon the free and unimpeded flow of rich information throughout the organization. This essentially demolishes the traditional organization chart.

4. These organizations are largely without boundaries, existing instead with a network of interdependent relationships up the supply chain and down the distribution channel all the way to the end-user. All are enlisted into a *codestiny* relationship in which they commit themselves to one another toward a common goal.

5. This codestiny in turn demands a nearly unrestricted flow of information between the players as well as within each organization. Thus, a manufacturer might share new

product information with a supplier, which in turn shares its own pricing data with its customer. Meanwhile, distributors, retailers, and even the customer might be enlisted into the product's design, manufacture, and service.

6. All of this demands an unprecedented level of trust between all of the participants: between labor and management, between suppliers and vendors, and between customers and manufacturers. In the end, trust becomes the single most important factor in the success or failure of these enterprises.

Sound familiar? That's because the virtual corporation and the Informed Sales Force share the same philosophical underpinnings. In fact, ISF is the last great link in the creation of this new business model. And, like the transformations occurring in manufacturing, management and marketing, it has the same needs: a reversal of the decision-making process to give control to the individual salesperson and his or her customer, the free flow of any and all information pertinent to the sale, and, most of all, trust in the salesperson's ability to represent the company properly, make the right product configuration and pricing decisions in conference with the customer, and advance the company's long-term interests.

Sadly, most of the Sales Force Automation tools currently on the market are not only not designed for this new organizational model, but actually *reinforce the obsolete model*. Thus, many companies that think they are buying a cure for their problems are actually buying more of the disease.

But the reverse is also true, and just as pernicious. Companies that adopt the Virtual Selling model and move to-

ward a Total Sales Quality while still clinging to the old hierarchical top-down organization will, at best, be setting
themselves up for years of internal friction and misery.
This will be the corporate sales version of Alvin Toffler's
Future Shock: the tools themselves will demand changes of
their owners.

Some of these firms will literally tear themselves apart.
Others will limp along, devoting too much time and energy
to putting down revolts by a liberated sales force against an
entrenched corporate bureaucracy. The luckiest will find
themselves with an institutional insurgency—a dynamic,
informed sales force—that will slowly compel the rest of
the company to change with it.

Of course, the best scenario of all is one in which your
company sees the future and begins working toward this
new organization now. You don't need fancy computers to
start shifting decision making down through the organization and out into the sales offices. Nor do you need video
phones and teleconferencing to increase the levels of mutual trust within the organization. In fact, the only tools
you really need are the hearts and minds of management
and labor. Start building that structure now, and the hardware and software will largely select itself—and your Informed Sales Force will smoothly take its place as the
dynamo at the center of your virtual corporation.

Chapter 6

Finding the Facts

If you had a $25 million dollar piece of equipment in your factory, you wouldn't think twice about paying 5% a year to keep it fine tuned, yet companies argue for days about spending a few bucks to keep a $25 million sales team selling.
—Robert Boylan
Results Now, Inc.

We now have a clue to what technology a company must have to get on the Virtual Selling path to the realization of Total Sales Quality. But that knowledge only gives us the vehicle, not the destination. We also need to understand how all that technology should be *used*.

So, this and the next few chapters will address in turn each of the key components of the sales process in order to develop a scenario for how each should properly function in an Informed Sales Force.

THE ENDLESS QUEST

The first and most obvious feature of modern sales is the endless search for information. Before you can even know *what* the information is (much less whether it is relevant or useful), you first must know *where* it is, *who* has got it, *why* they have it, and *which* technique (borrow, cajole, threaten, beg, etc.) will best serve to wrestle that information from its owner.

In other words, the "Five W's" of investigative journalism and private detection have now become the operating rules of salesmanship. And as any salesperson knows too well, in the labyrinthine Kafkaesque world of the modern corporation, the sales process can be even harder than it sounds. As often as not, you never do find the right person with the information you need; or, you find the right person, but even he or she can't locate the item in the billions of bytes of information scattered on disk drives throughout the organization.

Thus, in our so-called Information Age many salespeople, despite being armed with laptop computers and cellular telephones, are forced to fly as blindly as they did before computers. That's bad enough, but when the sales force loses its sight so does the company.

You don't have to look far for examples of blind corporations. Typically they share one of two traits:

•*They Are Dazed and Confused:* These are companies, big and small, old and new, that have been blind-sided by a sudden and profound change—a paradigm shift, to use the popular new term—in their market. They don't see it com-

Finding the Facts

ing and don't have any idea how to cope with the shift when it arrives. Blacksmiths, wheelwrights, photo development laboratories and small print shops are all classic examples of industries that have been blindsided by sudden technological shifts. Beyond having a worldly and well-read senior management, there is little that can be done to protect firms from such an unexpected fate.

However, especially in high tech, there is a variant on this kind of blindness that does have an obvious remedy. These victims are companies that are stunned, and usually destroyed, by market shifts. The story is as old as electronics: a new technology makes possible a new type of product . . . and the sudden demand for that product, combined with its high value-added pricing, sets off a land rush of companies, new and old, leaping into the market to stake their claims.

Over the last thirty years, these explosions have occurred in calculators, digital watches, video games, personal computers, disk drives, office software, on-line services, and dozens of other industries. And the scenarios are almost always the same: from a couple of pioneering companies, the market swells to scores of competitors. (In 5.25-inch Winchester disk drives in the early 1980s there were an estimated 150 players.) Finally a critical mass is reached, demand peaks, and prices fall precipitously. By industry veterans this is called a shake-out, and when the dust settles in a year or two perhaps no more than a half-dozen companies will be left. The rest will either disappear or, if they are lucky, will be bought by the winners.

This cycle occurs over and over—yet each time the

losers always seem stunned (that is, dazed and confused) that the bottom could have fallen out so quickly. They were already in free fall before they knew the bubble had burst. Who could have known?

Actually, their salespeople knew all too well. Many knew within hours after the first of their competitors slashed prices. But management wasn't listening. And, lacking support from above, these salespeople watched helplessly as orders evaporated. The smart ones began printing out their resumes.

• *They Are Lurching Companies:* This second type of blindness almost exclusively occurs at very big, established companies that have grown so big and complacent that they have allowed their information lines either to expand into chaos or to become sclerotic with disuse.

The problem begins when these firms too get hit by an unexpected technological change or market shift. However, unlike the dazed and confused firms, these companies are simply too big to sink immediately. Rather, these corporate *Titanics* hit their iceberg but the impact barely registers on the top decks. Frantic calls from the engine room go unheeded because the speaking tubes to the bridge have long since rusted out. Only after the steerage is flooded, the engine room threatened, and the passengers racing around in panic, does the ship's command realize that something is amiss.

Officers and crew, all experienced hands, now do their best, but the same atrophied systems stymie them at every step. It is impossible to learn anything about what is going on below that is less than twenty minutes old—but now events are occurring every two minutes. The crew can only react to old news, and their moves are exactly the wrong ones for what just happened. The ship lurches back and forth, the passengers dive into the sea . . .

We've all seen Lurching Companies. Twenty years ago it was the major Detroit automakers. In the 1980s it was DEC and Texas Instruments. And in the 1990s, most remarkably, it has been IBM. Each was a giant, arrogant company that dominated its market so completely as to be synonymous with it. Each had an enormous information-gathering apparatus that was allowed to wither until it became a vestigial part of the enterprise. Headquarters, not the field, always knew best. The model worked well as long as the status quo obtained.

But when the inevitable shift came, in the form of Japanese competitors, workstations, and mass market PCs, they were unable to adapt. In a twist on Rosabeth Moss Kanter's felicitous phrase, these giants couldn't dance. They didn't know what was happening until after it happened—and it was happening everywhere: new competitors, shifts in customer satisfaction requirements and promotion effectiveness, new trends in pricing, reordering, demographics and most of all, products. Like generals trained to fight the last war, the executives of these companies found themselves on the battlefield with the wrong uniforms, the wrong weapons, the wrong tactics . . . and facing an ominous opponent. In a panic, but always a step behind the competition, these leaders sent their companies lurching in one wrong direction after another (Do we stick with big cars in case the gas crisis ends? Or build little ones? Do we copy the Japanese or the Europeans? Do customers now want performance or economy?)—always operating from wrong or incomplete information.

In the end each of these companies survived not just because they were big enough to absorb the hits, but because, in desperation, they gave up on their failed information networks and created, often *ad hoc*, brand new ones. But by then these giants had lost billions of dollars, damaged the lives of the thousands of employees they laid off, wounded the trust of those who remained, and hurt forever their relations with customers. How much easier it would have been if GM had listened when its reps first talked about losing customers to Honda, or if IBM had not ignored its salespeople when they first noted the trend away from corporate computer centers.

INFORMATION IS POWER

Moore's Law all but predicts that we will see more and more dazed and confused companies lurching about on their way to oblivion. Like big but slow-moving, strong but dim-witted creatures faced with an oncoming glacier, these companies will become extinct because their nervous systems won't be quick enough to adapt. They have run smack into the underlying dilemma of modern industry—which reads like this:

—*Who knows what the customer wants and what's really going on in the market?*
—Sales and customer service.
—*Who makes the decisions about what the company will do?*

—The executive staff for business, marketing for product definition, and engineering for product design.
—*How often do these groups exchange notes?*
—Almost never.

Four hundred years ago, the man who initiated the technological revolution, Francis Bacon, wrote that "Knowledge is power." As Lord Chancellor of England under an unpredictable king, he knew a lot about bureaucratic inertia and arrogant executives.

In our time, knowledge is information. And in that light, Bacon's words have never been more true. Increasingly, products and services are displaying a growing information component, if they are not replaced by information altogether. Many products now "learn" as they are used, adapting to the user for maximum performance. One need only look at the "software" component of everything from personal computers to VCRs to home appliances and automobiles to recognize that the physical components are shrinking in importance. There are currently 10 *billion* microprocessors and miscontrollers in use in the world, their little silicon brains adding intelligence to every part of our lives.[1]

In the future the value of a corporation will be best measured by

- its knowledge of its customers
- its knowledge of markets
- its knowledge of its own products.

Therein will lie the company's competitive power.

It follows that as a corporation needs to interchange

more and more data with strategic partners, suppliers, and distributors; as it adds more intelligence into its products and then harvests what those products have learned from use; and as it has to gain ever-increasing understanding of its customers to supply them with mass-customized products, the corporation itself becomes less a collection of buildings and equipment and more a concatenation of vast stores of information. It is precisely this change that lies behind Moriarty and Swartz's discovery that "the price a product can command is less a reflection of raw materials and labor than of marketing-related services."[2]

This new organizational evanescence is behind the notion of a virtual corporation: with many of the employees at home, its production scattered around the world and up and down the supply-distribution chain, and its products and services defined less by what they are than by what the customer wants them to be, the modern corporation begins to turn into pure information.

Well, not entirely pure. There will still be employees (though fewer), especially salespeople. And these salespeople will typically find themselves not, as in the past, short of sales support data, but buried in useless mounds of it. That pile of worthless sales leads on the modern salesperson's desk is a hint of what is to come. So is that closet full of obsolete brochures. So, for that matter, are the inch-thick printouts of meaningless statistics that now show up on managers' desks once each month. The company of the near future will be awash in this kind of stuff. Meanwhile, *somewhere* out there, like diamonds in the mud, will be the information that counts, that creates success, that *confers power.*

Finding the Facts

Where do you find that information? You begin by understanding that some individuals in an organization gain power by hoarding information. Thus, every company has hidden caches of useful knowledge. One might be in the head of a particular product manager, another may be on the computer down at the loading dock, another may be in the notebook of the one guy in the lab who really understands all the bugs in the new product. Great salespeople are the folks who have found these caches and know how to raid them—a skill that it is not in their interest to share with anyone else. After all, salespeople are valued for personally knowing everything, not for sharing their knowledge. And, because this vital information is not shared, it cannot be leveraged, it enjoys no economies of scale. The company is essentially held hostage by a few clever individuals. Information gathering, storage and dissemination, which, by Moore's Law, should become cheaper as technology becomes more powerful, remain at best a fixed cost.

So what happens instead? Companies try to make up for their lack of access to their own knowledge bases through a number of compromise methods, most of them developed out of desperation:

• *Story-telling:* This is a leftover from the old days of selling. You might imagine that in an era when we can send the equivalent of a book around the world in a millisecond that this would be obsolete, yet a cynical view of modern business would hold that most market research is based upon anecdote. The sales rep hears something from a customer and passes it on to his boss ("Fred over at Acme kinda hinted that our competitor, Gizmo, is low-balling bids.

Maybe Gizmo's hurting these days"), who in turn passes up to senior management ("We're hearing reports that Gizmo is having a bad quarter.") Certainly there is nothing wrong with anecdotal information—no electronic system will ever be sufficiently rich to capture all the nuances of subjective human experience. But when myth and rumor become your primary market research tools, you are in trouble.

•*Snapshot*: Marketing and product design operations often try to supplement anecdotal information by conducting customer surveys. This method looks more systematic and scientific, but that is an illusion. Most customer surveys are designed to reinforce the manufacturer's own current biases or to paper over bad news, or else they simply ask the wrong questions. But even when they are done right, customer surveys are merely snapshots; they capture only one moment in time. Because they are expensive and time-consuming, customer surveys are rarely done. Thus, over a period of years, the company obtains at most a handful of nearly random, unconnected data points that do little to predict where the customer is now, or where it is going.

And what little it does show is usually hoarded by the marketing department . . .

•*Field of Dreams:* When all else fails, and it often does, the company essentially gives up and unconsciously admits that it has no idea what the market wants. Marketing then redefines the product based upon gut feeling, and engineering designs the product for itself. The overall attitude is "Build it and they will come."

Sometimes this so-called "next bench syndrome" actually works. It did for the Apple I and the HP-35 calculator. But most of the time it is an unmitigated disaster. Sales knows. Just count the glum faces at a sales conference during the next new-product presentation. But complaining won't do any good: sales will be ordered to sell this latest work of genius or else—and will be blamed when it can't.

• *Bull Run:* This compromise usually comes from Executive Row. It says that if you don't know what the market wants right now, then look at what it used to want and extrapolate from there. This technique may have worked in the Middle Ages, when little changed for centuries at a time. But these days, when everything seems to be zigzagging into the future, such "educated guesswork" is really just dumb luck. It is the equivalent of those generals at the beginning of the Civil War who, trained at West Point to fight in the 50-year-old Napoleonic style despite the rise of radically improved weaponry, turned their battlefields into meat grinders.

Of course, if you do manage by some fluke to actually hit the target you will be declared a genius and you'll be on the cover of *Business Week.*

• *Cherchez le Data:* Some companies have the courage to admit to themselves that they've lost control of their knowledge base. Unfortunately, most then take off in the wrong direction in pursuit of a solution. The critical mistake they make is to confuse information with data—that is, facts grounded in experience and need versus raw statistics that may or may not have any relevance. They burn huge sums of money installing equipment and subscribing to market watch services that provide them with massive quantities of raw data.

Then, when that data proves unusable, they conclude not that it is fundamentally misguided, but that it wasn't gathered well enough. So they go out and hire consultants to tell them why their data isn't any good. Now they've wasted their money twice, because the consultant has been hired to fix their current system, not to tell them to throw it all out. They are now trapped in a vicious circle, spending more and more of the company's gold chasing a bad initial investment.

HORDES OF INFORMATION

What then should a company pursuing Total Sales Quality do to find the useful facts that lie buried within it?

Go back to first principles. The goal of TSQ is to achieve a perfect correspondence between qualified leads and sales. This is only possible if we have a profound understanding of our customers, the state of the market, and the capabilities of our own company's products. These are the same three measures described earlier that will be used to measure the value of companies in the future.

This is not a minor point: it underscores the direct correlation between Total Sales Quality and the fate of organizations in the information age. It argues that having an Informed Sales Force is critical to corporate success.

These three metrics also hint at a rule regarding corporate information. It is as follows:

Finding the Facts

Anything that helps a company improve its common information on customers, markets, and products is beneficial. Anything that hinders the accumulation of this information is destructive to the company.

What does that mean? For one thing, it means that no individual, group, or department in an organization should be rewarded for hoarding information. On the contrary, even if they are sales superstars, they should be treated in the same way as any other employee would be whose behavior threatens the company's survival.

Yellow Freight, when it first installed its sales information system, ran into just such resistance from some of its best salespeople. Beginning in 1994, the shipping giant had armed 800 salespeople and managers at its 510 terminals with laptop computers equipped with high-speed modems and given the recipients extensive training in their use. The system has proven highly effective—increasing the time Yellow Freight's salespeople are in front of customers by 30 percent—but initially it was met with distrust. Acceptance of the equipment was not the problem; rather it was the unwillingness of some salespeople to share information with their peers.

"Some of the salespeople have had to be coached and prodded to enter in good, solid, accurate information. And there is some possessiveness," Yellow Freight's Denver rep Mike Holtzer told *Sales & Marketing Management*. "But the game plan is changed. They've got to share it. When they make a call, they've got to enter the information and be thorough. That's information we can all use."[3]

This rule also demands that the communication of information within an organization be two-way. The critical phrase here is "common information." Two-way communication cannot be construed as the old-fashioned model of raw data flowing up to management and being answered by commands and orders on their way down to the field. The model is only efficient if all parties in the organization have full access to all information of common interest.

Says sales automation consultant George W. Colombo:

> Every sales department has its own fingerprint, and any system has to be responsive to the needs of the people who are going to use it. That is one of the reasons why sales is late in coming to re-engineering.[4]

Now, obviously, perfect information sharing amongst every office in a company is an ideal. There will always be private records, secure files, and unshared work in progress. But, like TSQ itself, the model is convergent, and the ultimate goal remains unlimited access by all players. Needless to say, achieving that kind of total access will require most companies to rethink their entire IS philosophy. Unlimited access will require very sophisticated networks capable of carrying very rich multimedia information to a great number of nodes. That means big client-server systems, replication servers, and high-performance personal systems . . . all of the equipment we talked about in the last chapter. In other words, a good ISF program requires a great IS program. Ideally, sales information becomes synonymous with management information, manufacturing information, and product design information.

But won't all this input produce a lot of redundancy as multiple sources—say, a number of different sales reps— input roughly the same data? Sure. But redundancy is only a bad thing when you have insufficient memory or inefficient cataloguing. If you've got those limitations covered, then redundancy is actually useful because it confirms facts, transforming data into information. So the answer is to have an information network powerful enough to identify complementary inputs from diverse sources, locate contradictions and commonalties, then organize them together for universal access.

We also need that system to be flexible enough to store, but segregate, subjective anecdotal information in such a way that it is part of the file but yet held separate until more confirmation arrives. Why keep the anecdotal stuff when we've got hard facts? Because the world is a messy place; perfect truth is usually unknowable, so we must retain the subjective, even irrational components as well.

A good example of a company using technology to find an innovation solution to all four sides—corporate data and sales information, objective facts and subjective notes—is Parke-Davis, the prescription drug division of Warner-Lambert. Parke-Davis armed its 1,300 salespeople with pen-based computers in 1992.[5]

Parke-Davis faced two challenges in the field. The first was research. A test of a major new pharmaceutical may involve 2,000 or more subjects. In the past, researchers would interview these subjects, laboriously fill out forms by hand, then mail or fax them in to headquarters, where the data would then be retyped into the computer. Using the same pen computers as the sales force, the researchers now simply write in the data and it is instantly transmitted to the company. The result, Parke-Davis estimates, is savings of as much as $1 million per day as the data-entry process is cut by weeks or months. And that in turn may also mean saving some lives.[6]

Meanwhile, the sales force faces two tasks. The first, demanded by federal law, is to get a signature from every doctor with whom the rep leaves a drug sample. This is usually done on the run and is a bureaucratic nightmare. With the pen computers, the rep can now just get a quick electronic signature and send it in.

There's more. In that brief encounter with the doctor, the rep needs to make a case. There is little time for presentation. "They walk in and out of doctors' offices, often catching them on the fly, and don't have time to set up screens," says Rich Cella, Parke-Davis' IS director.[7] The answer, then, is to custom-tailor the presentation beforehand, limiting the sales scenarios to those the doctor will most likely prefer. That's why Parke-Davis now supports those computers with extensive data bases that combine the data from the field tests described above, and also track the doctor's past purchase history. This last is most interesting because Parke-Davis' system is designed to detect subtle nuances in each doctor's prescription preferences.[8]

BEHIND THE INFORMATION

We have our rule, but we aren't done yet. Our new information system requires two more features, purpose and timeliness.

•*Purpose:* By definition, a system must be systematic, and when we are talking about a sales information system, it is not enough that the architecture alone be well designed. Recent business history is replete with stories of elegant computer networks that didn't do what they were supposed to.

You cannot collect data without an underlying strategy. If you do, you end up with a mass of disconnected random data. Without selection criteria, you approach this data not knowing where to start or what to throw out. Nothing is extraneous, yet everything is.

Conversely, there is also a danger in attacking data with a narrow agenda. Draw your focus too tight and you will almost always find what you are looking for—even if it is New Coke or the PCjr. Set out to confirm your prejudices and you will find ample support—look at how the Democrats and Republicans always have poll results that support their positions.

So how do you maintain control without biasing your results? If there was a simple answer the world would be using it. However, there is a satisfactory, if not perfect, answer. It's the one found in democracy, notably in the first amendment to the U.S. Constitution. The more you allow the free flow of information and access to that information, the more likely it is that falsehoods and irrelevancies will be identified and exposed. Furthermore, the useful information will find those who need it, while worthless data will languish. Most of all, mission-critical information will be accessible in time to those whose future depends upon it.

And that, of course, is precisely the sales information system described in this chapter. Will this kind of information democracy survive in a modern corporation? That depends upon how well the players trust one another. To succeed and endure, a sales information system must:

- "know" what is important and sift out extraneous data
- gather information continuously and with a defining goal in view
- be mutually beneficial to all the parties involved
- be central to the way business decisions are made at every level of the company and its strategic partners.

The model for such a system as is described in this chapter accomplishes these requirements better than any other. But just as it must have a purpose to succeed, so too must the organization it serves. And if the organization's real purpose is not to increase market share, sales, and profits, but to enforce social stratification and accumulate individual power, then no information can succeed.

- *Timeliness:* The temporal factor is just as important as the architectural one. We might have the most sophisticated IS program on earth, but if it is not continuously updated and its files not immediately accessible, then we will find ourselves lurching around in the Bull Run mode, reacting to old news and fighting the last war.

Some of the better sales information systems in place today try to update their files on a daily basis. For example, in 1991 cereal giant Kellogg put in place a sales system that armed its sales reps with Grid pen-based hand-held computers and Fastech sales information software.[9]

The Grid computers weren't cheap, but Kellogg justified the investment because its current information apparatus (bubble forms that the reps filled in like SAT answer sheets) was so slow—six to eight weeks to process—that the company was losing its ability to keep up with changes in market demand, especially in light of the fact that a new cereal typically has just 90 days to prove itself to retailers. Said Richard Hirsh, Fastech's vice president of marketing and sales, "The response time of the older [Kellogg] system made it almost impossible to get the kind of feedback needed to quickly find out which products were selling or not selling and to take appropriate action."[10]

With the new system, the Kellogg sales reps could write order and inventory figures right on the computer screen for storage—then, each night, plug the computer into a phone jack and use the machine's built-in modem to automatically transfer the data to Kellogg's central computer base. In the morning, the reps could download the updated files and head back out into the field.[11]

The Kellogg sales information system was an impressive accomplishment, one most companies today have yet to achieve. Yet it is a measure of how fast things are changing that the Kellogg system would be dangerously archaic for many companies today. File data once per day? For a global business, hourly currency fluctuations between countries could alone evaporate many of the profits on a deal by nightfall. Likewise, a customer needing assistance may have gone from anxious to worried to despair from one morning's request to the next morning's response. And a surfeit of inventory that led to a deal might be an empty warehouse by the time the order arrives that night.

What many companies need today are sales information update functions that occur *hourly*—say, by dialing into the home office computers via the nearest telephone line. That's what Hewlett-Packard is doing. Its sales reps, each armed with a laptop computer, portable printer, and cellular phone, can directly access HP corporate data bases to obtain up-to-the-minute data on pricing, availability, and customer order status. The HP rep can also contact data bases containing the customer's profile, as well as leads and prospects.[12]

According to Liz Faracik, HP's European sales and marketing service program manager, an immediate benefit of this system when it was installed in 1989 was that reps were spending more time with customers—up from two to three calls per day—primarily because they no longer had to waste time in company meetings (down 40 percent) or visiting the office to get answers. Meanwhile, order performance was immediately up 10 percent.[13]

CLOSING THE LOOP

You don't have be a prophet to see where the trend is going: to real-time/broadband data access from wherever the salesperson is. That will require wireless telecom, even satellite-based systems. And if data access is going to be instantaneous (and remember the rule about all communications being two-way and universal) then all responses from the company must be instantaneous as well. No more having the sales force file records and requests, then manufacturing taking 24 hours to reply and marketing using up two weeks preparing a report.

Spin out that thread and you realize that the only way the company will be able to react instantaneously is if it has a similar relationship with its suppliers, distributors, and strategic partners. That pulls the entire sphere of corporate relationships into our information system.

And we're not done yet. The logical conclusion of all of this is that the ultimate participant in this web of relationships, the customer, almost must become part of the network. How? Through the salesperson. By helping design and order, with the salesperson's assistance, the product or service he or she will buy, the customer becomes both supplier and consumer.

We have thus closed the loop. At the beginning of this book it was noted that the salesperson is the one company employee who contributes to both sides of the balance sheet. Now, with Virtual Selling, for the first time the architecture of the corporate information system mirrors that fact. And, by working to close the system, we once again move toward Total Sales Quality.

Next let's see what happens at that closure point, where the informed salesperson meets the engaged customer.

Chapter 7

Total Quality Marketing

No part of the modern company will undergo more change than marketing.

That much most people know. But what is often missed is that this change will twist traditional marketing operations in two, accelerating one half (traditional sales marketing) down its current path, while forcing the other half (marketing communications) to completely transform itself into something entirely different from what it is today.

What's more, these two branches will then experience their own convergence comparable to that taking place in sales. For consistency's sake, one might call this process *total quality marketing.* The goal of this process has already been named—*maxi-marketing*—in 1988 by Stan Rapp and Tom Collins in their book of the same name.[1]

"Maxi-marketing" actually is something of a misnomer, suggesting as it does an expansion of marketing's territory.

But what Rapp and Collins actually identified was a new model of marketing's function in a world where technology and communications have rendered traditional mass marketing obsolete.

In this, Rapp and Collins were following a trail first blazed a decade before by Alvin Toffler, who, in *The Third Wave*, coined the term *demassification*. As Toffler described it:

> The mass market has split into ever-multiplying, ever-changing sets of mini-markets that demand a continually expanding range of options, models, types, sizes, colors and customizations.[2]

Toffler's clarion call about the death of the mass market and the rise of demassification (or mini-marketing, targeted marketing, maxi-marketing, niche marketing, narrowcasting ... there have been nearly as many names as authors) was picked up and refined by business theorists as diverse as Peter Drucker, John Naisbitt and Tom Peters. Whatever the style, the message is essentially the same—a cascade of cause and effect:

1. *Technology is changing products and services.* The presence of intelligence within products and in the creation of services gives these products and services an unprecedented adaptability to the needs of the user. But in the process of adapting, these products and services stop being of a common type or form, and become individually unique.

2. *Technology is changing customers.* Users of these products and services, recognizing and enjoying this change, will begin to demand more; increasingly becoming resistant to

nonadaptive, undifferentiated mass market goods. A new form of sales must be developed to reach these customers.

3. *Technology is changing manufacturing.* As demand increases for these adaptive products and services, manufacturing will have to become adaptive as well, adopting a new philosophy of "mass customization," which means mass production in lots as little as one unit. This will mean revamping production by adding Just-In-Time inventory techniques, Total Quality Manufacturing, work teams and high levels of automation. In the meantime, products and services will increasingly become synonymous as both exhibit such common features as an inability to be inventoried and creation at the point of delivery.

4. *Technology is changing corporations.* This revolution won't be confined to the factory or sales. The extraordinary speed and agility demanded by these new "virtual products" will force companies to reorganize into "virtual corporations," invert their power structures, install massive information systems, and develop unprecedentedly tight relationships with suppliers, distribution/retail channels, and customers.

5. *Technology is changing delivery systems.* Within such virtual corporations, information will flow upward and products downward, and the faster and richer the information flow the more competitive and effective the counterflowing delivery process. This will mean common data interchange networks and extraordinary degrees of access by all players. And, because the finished products will themselves have high levels of information content, they will also become information-gathering nodes for the network.

6. *Technology is changing marketing.* As the information-gathering apparatus for the organization, marketing finds

itself in the pivotal position. It will have to develop sophisticated data acquisition and storage systems to cope with the huge amount of information continuously gathered to satisfy the customer with truly customized products. At the same time, marketing must be the "face" of this enormous multicorporation superstructure in its contacts with the customer, insuring that the customer's dealings with this supplier/manufacturer/distributor/retailer network are satisfying and enduring.

THE LOST CAUSE

In other words, marketing is now the engine of the corporation. And its interdependence with sales becomes greater than ever. Sales as the focal point of the new organization cannot function, nor maintain the tight and enduring relationship it needs with customers, without extraordinary levels of support from marketing. Virtual Selling exists on information. It will consume it in enormous quantities. Manufacturing will provide some of that information; so will senior management, suppliers, and the distribution channel. The sales force will also gather information of its own.

But, by far, the preponderance of that information will come from marketing. If marketing fails in this task, sales will falter as customers lose trust, and the company will be at risk.

When faced with this enormous, but nebulous, responsibility, the natural reaction is overkill. After all, the reasoning goes, better to go overboard than to come up short. One can see this in corporations everywhere. Computer networks are put in place, subscriptions to market services beefed up, and every note from every department in the company is stuffed into data bases and regularly dumped out in gigantic reports filled with thousands of undigested scraps of worthless data.

This marketing department regurgitation winds up on desks everywhere from Executive Row to the field sales offices . . . and there it sits, unread, until it is thrown out to make room for the next report.

Why is this happening? Because marketing too is trapped in an old, divergent model. As with sales, this inertia is a product of history. What we now call marketing was a product of the "scientific" revolution that swept U.S. industry in the early years of the 20th century. It affected every part of the corporation, from time-motion studies in the factory to organizational theory at headquarters. Until that time, marketing didn't really exist. Rather, new product sales strategies largely arose from a gut sense of what the market wanted and how those desires might change.

Marketing itself was something of a stepchild of statistics and behaviorism. The idea, held to this day, was that by a combination of demographics, statistical sampling, focus testing, and customer feedback, one could develop a reasonably accurate profile of the average customer and his or her tastes. With this knowledge, R&D could develop new products, marketing devise new advertising campaigns, collateral material and promotions, and the field develop new sales pitches . . . all with reasonable expectation that their efforts would find a receptive audience.

Initially this worked well, because the marketplace, much of it still new to the Industrial Revolution, was comparatively static in its desires. However, as educational levels rose, and new technologies such as the telephone, automobile, and then radio became pervasive, this static demand became increasingly dynamic. Now, marketing was faced not only with a marketplace that was perpetually evolving, but was also regularly being handed innovative new products for which a market didn't yet exist.

A WORLD OF ABUNDANCE

Keeping tabs on the changing marketplace demanded real-time, continuous polling of customers. Just as technology created this situation, it also helped solve it. Computers, scanners, and high-speed telecommunications allowed for the gathering of inventory data at the point of sale; warranty cards and questionnaires could be stored and collated by the millions by large computers; and demographic data could be purchased from outside sources (researchers, the federal government, other companies) and downloaded directly into the customer's files.

In order to handle all of this information a new profession was created, Management Information Systems (MIS), which injected the computer room manager and the system analyst as a kind of technological insurgent into the very heart of the enterprise.

The second task, that of creating demand for a new technology, compelled the creation of a new wing on marketing: marketing communications, which became the home of some retargeted older operations, including public relations, advertising, collateral and technical publications. The job of these operations, and the professionals who filled them, increasingly became that of constructing demand for soon-to-be-available new products and services.

For PR, this meant raising consciousness by convincing the press to validate the new technology by reporting on it; for advertising and collateral, it meant appealing to desire, high and low, through mass market campaigns, and for publications, it meant the creation of flyers, brochures, and manuals that bridged the gap between what the customer knew and what the new technology demanded.

Despite the radical changes that occurred in marketing between the static and dynamic eras, there was the common thread of *scarcity of information*. Despite all of their efforts, companies basically flew blind most of the time when creating and selling new products. There simply wasn't enough research, testing, focus panel, customer profile or survey data available when it was needed to make crucial product development decisions. Thus, the primary task of marketing for a century was to *get more data*. Spend more on market research consultants, on computers, on data input devices for the field, on direct mail questionnaires . . . anything to get that next incremental bit of data about the market.

That philosophy of scarcity carries over to this day, even though we now live in an era of terabyte data bases and nearly infinite sources of raw data. A dearth of raw data is the least of our concerns. Unfortunately, except for a few cases, corporate marketing has yet to cope with this change.

The result is that, whereas twenty or thirty years ago added market data was a competitive advantage, today it can actually be a *disadvantage*. Like the survivor of a famine who can't stop eating long after abundance has returned, corporate marketing keeps cranking out more and more reports long after the rest of the company has stopped reading them.

This would merely be an expensive waste except that buried in that data is often information critical to the future of the company. But that information never gets read because the natural human response to information overload is to simply shut down—which is precisely what is happening on Executive Row, at the factory, in the lab, and out at the sales office (remember the mountains of response cards?).

This increasing indifference to the work of marketing in turn creates a vicious cycle. Marketing breaks its back to put out a 75-page management "summary" each week . . . and management never reads it. Marketing spends hundreds of thousands of dollars on an advertising campaign that produces thousands of query cards . . . and the sales force tosses them in the trash. Then, when revenues slump and the company misses a shift in customer demand, who gets blamed? Marketing. Which then redoubles its efforts to gather even more unusable, unread data.

A VOICE UNHEARD

That's the information-gathering side. A comparable crisis is taking place in marketing communications. The old model of manipulative mass advertising and "shotgunned" press releases to the widest possible audiences is losing its potency. One reason is that the audience has become more sophisticated—it's been years since consumers sat in slack-jawed wonder and belief at the latest claims about whiter whites, better cars, and tastier snacks. By the same token, most readers realize that a print advertisement cannot be trusted and that, while the editorial copy next to that ad may be more honest, it can only be depended upon for information, not value judgments.

Obviously, corporations still blithely spend hundreds of billions of dollars each year on mass-market advertising—witness the million-dollar-per-minute rates for commercials during the Super Bowl—but by nearly every measure, they are getting less and less for their investment.

Mass marketing is failing precisely because of the cascade effect described above. By definition, mass marketing is the strategy of convincing consumers to buy largely homogeneous products produced in high volume by the traditional mass-production factory system. But these days consumers are demanding just the opposite; they expect the products they buy to be unique to their tastes and needs. The age of the product "model" is just about over. And that creates a fatal paradox: it is almost impossible to market personalized products through impersonal, mass market channels.

About all that is possible through these channels is to market general capabilities—witness the growing number of "infomercials" and instructional ads—and hope the potential customer will take the time to actually read or watch this complicated message and then personally apply its possibilities.

There is a second complication developing here as well. It is that, historically, market communications has supported one-time sales. This will come as no surprise to anyone. When you use every promotional trick you know to sucker the potential customer in ... then turn that customer over to a salesperson who uses every selling trick he or she knows to close, you can hardly be planning to ever see that customer again.

That strategy worked in 1920 when the available U.S. market seemed endless. It even worked in 1985, when the global market seemed equally immense. But in the age of the infobahn and global competitors, the limits of any market are now shockingly close. Moreover, in this intense competition, few markets will remain uncontested for long—and that means the traditional bridge period of high margins will be shorter than ever. So it may take two or three product generations to see a real return.

But, if marcom's new task is to hold on to current customers, it is woefully unprepared. That full-page ad in *Time* isn't going to do it anymore—you don't need to introduce yourself to current customers. And if you follow this logic out even further, it becomes apparent that as more companies adopt this new philosophy they will bind up more and more of the customer base in enduring, tight relationships.[3]

Every corporate marcom department and every public relations and advertising agency is already caught in this paradigm shift, whether they know it or not. Most don't, which explains why thousands of advertisements are placed and millions of press releases are mailed out each year, all to no effect. Home mailboxes are filled with junk mail and editors' desks covered with press announcements that go unopened and unread on their way to the landfill. And there is more the next day. And the day after . . .

The most forward-thinking marketing communications professionals have identified this change and are working to move past it. A case in point is Regis McKenna. Once Silicon Valley's resident PR guru, five years ago McKenna suddenly announced that his agency was leaving the business it dominated and was moving into basic marketing. As McKenna explained it at the time, PR as a stand-alone business was obsolete; what companies needed now was help in rethinking their marketing from the ground up.

REWRITING THE RULES

Behind McKenna's decision was a recognition that the new ground rules of business implied by the virtual corporation demanded a new kind of marketing, both in terms of information acquisition and communications.

But finding that new model has proven problematic. It is one thing to recognize that the old techniques don't work, another to construct a suitable replacement. For example, the most obvious solution to the information acquisition problem—add more information acquisition systems—is also the worst one. So too, in communications, is the use of technology to refine the old tricks. This is CIM applied to marketing . . . with the same disastrous results.

But with the Virtual Selling model in place, we have an important clue to what to do with marketing. It is that whatever changes we make, marketing must produce results that feed into the TSQ system and supports the goal of an Informed Sales Force.

That suggests a rule:

Marketing's task in the corporation of the future is to support Total Sales Quality (TSQ) by locating, establishing and filling the narrowest possible sales funnel.

Total Quality Marketing

That's the information acquisition side. Here's the other half, dealing with marcom:

Marketing communications' new task is to represent the company in forming an enduring relationship with the customer, so as to determine that customer's changing needs before, during and after the purchase.

Obvious as each may sound, they are radical in their implications. The first rule, dealing with information acquisition, is defined by the phrase "narrowest possible sales funnel." If the absolute goal is to be a one-to-one correspondence between qualified leads and sales the huge amount of qualifying that needs to be done can hardly occur just before the leads hit the salesperson's desk. Rather, the filtering must begin at the start of the process, during the initial gathering of raw data, then continue all of the way through to final qualification.

This is the absolute antithesis of the wide-net principle being used by marketing today. It is the difference between piling 400 query cards in the salesperson's lap every week and handing that individual a 20-page profile of a single potential customer each morning.

The good news, especially for firms that have invested millions in computers and mass memory systems, is that this second, more potent, scenario requires pretty much the same hardware as the first. The difference instead is one of philosophy, and how that philosophy is made manifest in software.

At the heart of both models is *data-base marketing*, the use of computer technology to acquire, collate, and store vast collections of market-related data. As described by Edward Nash, author of *Database Marketing:*

Just by adding a phone number or a coupon to an ad and offering valuable information to the prospective customer, you can capture a name for the database. Unlike outside mailing lists, this is not just someone who should be interested in your product or service, but someone who actually is.

These prospects are like gold ore to the professional salesperson. The information you send them is educational and serves to amplify the sales message of an advertisement . . . It is the beginning of a relationship and leads not just to a sale but to long-term repeat business . . . it is the marketing world's missing link between the past and the future.[4]

As described by Rapp and Collins, data-base marketing is the inevitable result of Moore's Law colliding with information gathering:

Thanks to the computer, detailed profiles of millions of prospects and customers can be developed using geographic, demographic, and psychographic characteristics and buying history. Special products, services and offers can be tailored to selected segments of the database to increase both return on investment and customer satisfaction . . .

Because the cost of accessing data has fallen so swiftly, many people in marketing don't fully comprehend what database marketing can mean and what it can do. In 1973 it cost $7.14 to access 1000 bits of information; 1000 bits equals about 20 words of data—about enough to record a customer's name, address, and purchase. Today it costs about a penny to do the same thing.[5]

That was in 1988. Thanks to Moore's Law, the figure is now about one hundredth of a cent. Unfortunately, thanks to the wrong-headed open-ended model, too often the cost-savings have still been used to gather that 1000 bits—but now on 714,000 people for the price it took to record just one in 1973. Far better would it be to have all 714 million bits being used to locate, close and then keep for life just one potential customer.

Rapp and Collins recognized some of this. From Toffler, they took as their premise that technology was demassifying markets and once-monolithic markets were beginning to splinter into hundreds of submarkets created by rapidly changing customer tastes. As a result, they argued, the traditional techniques of mass marketing could only fail because they didn't address the specific new needs of each of these splinter markets.

So Rapp and Collins proposed their new "maxi-marketing" model, which consisted of nine steps that carried through three phases: reaching the prospect, making the sale, and developing the relationship. This book would call them information acquisition and the sales funnel, Virtual Selling, and marketing communications.

Of the three steps Rapp and Collins saw in reaching the prospect, just one, *maximized targeting*, is pertinent.[6] Here the authors show an early understanding that data-base marketing should be as much an exclusive as an inclusive process:

> Our working definition here is that targeted marketing is the art and science of identifying, describing, locating and contacting one or more groups of prime prospects for whatever you are selling . . . In today's marketplace, if you don't know who, what, and where your true prospects are, or if you fail to go after them as individuals, you will lose ground to competitors who do.[7]

Nowadays, identifying, locating, and contacting prospective customers is not the challenge it was even a decade ago. Today you can find and get in touch with every prospective customer in the industrialized world—and most of them in the rest of the world. But the real challenge is: what are you going to do with them after you've found them? In the second sentence, Rapp and Collins get it right—though probably not to the degree they could have imagined at the time. To truly go after prospects as "individuals" will require an individualized, customized, sales program.

Call this the *customer information pyramid*. What it means is that as the sales funnel narrows toward the sale, the knowledge needed about that customer increases. But more than that, the steeper the sides of the sales funnel (as in the TSQ philosophy) the shallower the walls of the customer information pyramid. In other words, to get to the perfect world of one-to-one correspondence between prospects and leads, you would need almost infinite quantities of information about the customer ... that is, the customer would have to sell to itself, assisted by the salesperson. That is, of course, the very definition of Virtual Selling.

The role of a marketing information program now becomes clear: *to carry the prospective customer to a level of trust in the relationship such that the customer will assume responsibility, with the salesperson's help, for self-closing.*

REDESIGNING THE FUNNEL

The presence of the customer information pyramid means the end of traditional marketing. This has always been true, but until recently the limitations on gathering that information have camouflaged the fact. Only now is the information grid sufficiently rich to make the situation obvious.

It is also now clear that the customer information pyramid also spells doom even to data-base marketing as we've come to know it. The reason is simple: you can't provide the huge numbers of prospective customers with the individually customized marketing demanded by maxi-marketing. Why? Because if your ability to compete for customers depends not only upon vast quantities of information you've gathered on those customers, but also in enlisting them in the final steps of a virtual sale, then, even with Moore's Law, there will never be enough computing power or salespeople to provide this level of support. *If you start with wide-net marketing, you will never have enough resources to achieve Total Sales Quality for more than a tiny fraction of those you identify.*

What that suggests is that there are now two distinct scenarios for how marketing must construct the sales funnel in pursuit of TSQ:

The TSQ Funnel: In this model, marketing develops a narrow focused sales funnel. This is a two-stage funnel, wide at the top, then tightening quickly to a narrow channel that characterizes the process to the end. In practice, this would mean retaining the traditional wide-net process of gathering as many sales leads as possible (data-base marketing, query cards, mailing and subscription lists, etc.), then rigorously and immediately applying a series of filters (income, purchase patterns, demographics, psychological profiles, etc.) to narrow the list to a select few, which then become the subject of intense research, profiling, and marketing tool preparation.

Virtual Selling

QUALIFIED LEADS

Prospects

Customer Visits

Proposals

Forecasted Deals

SALES

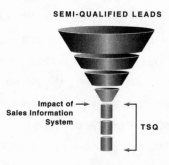

SEMI-QUALIFIED LEADS

Impact of →
Sales Information
System

TSQ

TSQ Funnel

The TSQ model, after all, is simply data-base marketing with a turbocharger. It identifies the biggest flaw of the traditional model—too much time and resources wasted on unlikely prospects—but cures it merely by speeding up the culling-out steps. That helps, but what it doesn't cure is the wastefulness of the past. The marketing department is still throwing out a wide net, contacting numerous potential customers, then throwing out most of them. As a result, the other problem identified earlier, the permanent loss of potential *future* customers through a dead-end current contact, is not resolved. It might even be aggravated.

But over time, as more and more customers become tightly bound in long-term relationships with the company, their presence—and the information they provide—will have two effects, both moving the company toward a focused, narrow model. First, as the company begins to develop massive files on every nuance of these customers' needs and desires, those customers will become their own individual sales funnels. Just as important, what is learned from these tightly bound customers will enable the company to begin prefiltering the marketplace to pinpoint likely prospects even before they are contacted. And, shared through the corporate IS network with R&D, manufacturing, service, and sales, this information will also orient the company's operations for the near future.

Thus, the marketing life cycle of a virtual corporation will likely be that, in its early years, it reaches out widely and uses the TSQ model to create its customer bases. After that, as it matures the relationship with these customers and reaches out to others just like them, the company moves more and more of the actual marketing operations to the sales force and even the customer itself.

Recognizing when to make these shifts will be the job of marketing management, which will need to cultivate not only an understanding of the market, but also the dynamics of the company itself. In the words of Allan J. Magrath, author of *How to Achieve Zero-Defect Marketing:*

... it is of great value for marketers periodically to rethink their efforts and reframe their marketing in terms of the developing issues and opportunities that surround it. Rethinking will sometimes jump start a whole new approach to growth, market share, new product, or corporate marketing priorities.[8]

A VOICE WITHIN

And what of marketing communications? Isn't it rendered superfluous by all of this? Not entirely. But Regis McKenna's decision now becomes more explicable: he didn't give up on public relations—his agency in fact still does its share of press relations—but only recognized that marcom would never again be a truly independent function. Instead, it would be a servant of marketing and thus, by extension, of sales.

This change is not especially obvious under a TSQ marketing regime. There, advertising will still be aimed at reaching the largest possible audience, public relations will still attempt to influence the creation of as many articles in as many publications as possible, and collateral will still produce publications aimed at the widest possible readership.

Still, there will be some subtle changes in a TSQ model, many of which we can already see taking place in many progressive companies. For example, to ease the fast filtering process demanded of marketing, marcom will be expected to slightly narrow the mouth of the sales funnel. In particular, advertising will reduce its use of mass-market venues and instead spend more of its placement dollars in vertical publications. It would also be asked to increasingly shift its content emphasis from emotional manipulation to presentations about capabilities, applications, etc.

PR will experience the same shift of emphasis. With the exception of shareholder relations, emphasis will move from story placement in general-interest publications to an even greater emphasis on trade publications, both in the company's own industry and in the vertical publications catering to key target markets. Ultimately, the focus will get even tighter, centering on cultivating opinion makers ("key influencers") such as newsletter editors, well-known technologists, and trend-setters.

Collateral, for its part, will find itself in more of a training role, through publications and point-of-sale materials acting as the first filter and the first instructor in training the prospect to become a competent customer.

But it is with the Virtual Selling model that these professions turn upside down. Now these outward-looking professions turn inward, their tasks changed from landing new customers to working with existing customers to make the mutual experience satisfying and enduring. Now advertising's job is to sell the customer base on what is coming next—and that means using new communications vehicles (videos, fliers, social events) as well as working with sales management to create compelling sales presentation tools. But most of all, sales will have to develop techniques to help marketing gather as much information as possible about these long-term customers.

PR too will find its outside activities introverted. There will still be press relations—to support stock prices, influence government policy, and keep customers feeling secure—but more and more PR's job will be to talk directly with customers. This likely means that PR will establish links with customers in much the way corporate communications talks with employees—through newsletters, magazines, videos, and training seminars—and add such other channels as computer bulletin boards, Internet Web Sites and direct mail.

Collateral will shift more and more to post-sales communications with existing customers, rather than pre-sales with prospects. As public relations will be directing much of this communication, collateral will likely provide the materials used by PR.

This shift will be very difficult for some corporate marcom departments. Though some professionals may embrace this new challenge, others may strenuously resist it as a threat to their competence. After all, twenty years of writing press releases isn't the best training for editing employee newsletters.

And there is yet another wrinkle in all this. If the company is going to grow and change and enter new markets, marcom, just like the rest of marketing, will have to be able to move back and forth between market focused versus customer focused techniques. Will that be possible? Can a single advertising copywriter or publicist or graphic artist switch back and forth without a diminishment in his or her skills? Will companies have to maintain two departments for each job? Or will they simply hold on to management in these areas and contract out the work as needed? And if they do this last, how will they maintain the close customer relationships they will need over the long term?

Total Quality Marketing

None of these questions has an easy answer. And that is why, in the years to come, during all the dislocations that will occur in sales as a result of the shift to Total Sales Quality, marketing too will need to re-engineer itself to fit the needs of Virtual Selling.

Chapter 8

Virtual Selling

There is no such thing as a "soft sell" and "hard sell." There is only "smart sell" and "stupid sell."
— *Charles Hendrickson Bower, 1958.*

All the pieces are in place now: the requisite hardware and software, the operating rules, the methodology of Virtual Selling, and the goal of Total Sales Quality.

But in the end, all that really counts is whether this immense and complex structure improves the productivity of the individual salesperson. After all the theory, the equipment, and the preparation, it all comes down to the moment when the salesperson sits down with the potential customer. This is the real test.

Chapter 3, "Making the Sale," surveyed how selling is currently done, and how the old model is increasingly

184

showing cracks and flaws as the nature of products, companies, and the marketplace change. This chapter revisits the moment in light of the new model to see how it "remakes" selling: what features it transforms, what it retains and what it abandons.

One thing that doesn't change is that selling is selling. It is still a four-step process of *qualification, presentation, configuration, and close.* What changes is the level of emphasis placed upon each of these steps. Let's look at each of these steps as they will function in an informed sales force.

TELLING THE STORY

For a decade, Marla Silbernagel, a salesperson at Waters Chromatography in Milford, Massachusetts, searched for more effective sales presentational materials to help her describe her company's complicated products (devices that measure the chemical components of liquids) to prospective customers.[1] She used overhead slides, charts, "anything I could get my hands on to make my presentations more effective. I would hoard brochures, handouts, anything that might enhance my presentations."[2] Even then, she was forced to carry stacks of three-ring binders.

By 1993, however, Silbernagel and the rest of Waters' 120-person sales force were carrying only color notebook computers. Everything in Silbernagel's stack of binders was now on a hard disk on her computer; but more than that, she can now personalize the result for each customer.

The manager behind the shift was Neal David, director of marketing systems for the company. For David, the challenge was to find a way to get all of the complex information about the company to the field and then the equally complex orders back to headquarters. Passing printed material back and forth just wasn't adequate anymore. In particular, what David concluded his company needed was a format to bring together all of the best presentations that had been created by company salespeople in the past, and the tools to enable those same salespeople to easily cut and paste those old presentations together to create new ones tailored for the sales opportunity at hand.

The result, using NEC notebook computers and Lotus Freelance Graphics software, is a library database which can be accessed at any time by company salespeople. "The sales rep does not have to create a new sales presentation every time," says David. "He can browse through what's available on the server and just detach one. [He] can also take part of a presentation, or parts of several, to make up a very dynamic presentation. Our customers have been impressed by what they've seen . . . sales calls are more effective now, and the sales cycle time—from the initial contact to the time the order is placed—has shortened significantly."[3]

Of late, David has been looking at bringing multimedia capabilities to the presentation process. "I'm ready for that," he says, "but I'm not sure everybody else is."[4]

In the meantime, the new system has transformed selling at Waters. A survey in early 1994 found that there were more than 600 users of the program throughout the company, all in *de facto* collaboration. In one celebrated instance, when a customer couldn't analyze a chemical sample with Waters equipment, Waters' own R&D lab did the test, then transmitted the results directly to the company salesman—who was sitting in the customer's office.[5]

Certainly the new program has changed the life of Marla Silbernagel: "I want to communicate to my customers the fact that I take their needs seriously and that I consider them individually," Sibernagel told *Selling* magazine, "Personalizing my presentations is a key factor in being able to do that ... [and] we get more business because we look more professional and because these tools make us more credible."[6]

As every good salesperson knows, selling is first and foremost a narrative art. Pitching a customer is really a form of storytelling, in which that customer is the protagonist of an heroic epic in which he or she buys the product or service and uses it to slay a threatening dragon (a production problem, an aggressive competitor, a dangerous professional peer) and lives happily every after (gets a promotion, increases profits, meets a production goal).

The presentation process thus becomes three steps:

1. Convince the customer of the threat or opportunity
2. Prove the superiority of what is being sold in answering that need
3. Present an appealing scenario of the positive results that will come from using that product or service.

Looking at these three steps it becomes evident that the narrative of sales is really composed of both empirical and subjective components. In other words, a salesperson must be deeply empathetic to the desires of the potential customer so as to weave a powerful, and personalized, tale—but also must have all the performance stats, market numbers, competitive data, and a catalog of product configurations at his or her fingertips to assuage those desires.

With the exception of a few Renaissance men, this kind of superior left-brain/right brain combination is rarely found in human beings. That's why some people go into the humanities and others into the sciences. And that's why salespeople rarely moonlight in research laboratories and scientists rarely go along on sales calls.

It is also why, when you look at a typical sales organization, you typically see *two* sales forces, not one. They may work out of the same sales offices and have the same titles, but salespeople almost always reside in one of two camps: *closers*, the so-called "natural salesmen," who rely on their wits (and resourcefulness) to make a sale; and *techies*, who rely on their encyclopedic knowledge of the products to convince (or bludgeon) the customer into a purchase.

If you want a simple explanation of why we need a new paradigm shift in sales you'll find it within this divided sales force. Neither side is adapted to modern business. In a world where intelligent products may come in as many configurations as there are customers, where trust becomes central, the charmer is both ill-prepared and unreliable. And, as relationship building becomes as important as product capabilities, the techie is completely at sea.

The answer then is to devise presentation systems that complement the unique skill set of each salesperson. The sales force automation model has failed largely because it has given this presentation capability a lower priority than information gathering and dissemination. The Virtual Selling model, because it inverts the process, now puts the salesperson first and in control.

But in this context, what does that mean?

Look at our information-system model again. Leaving aside for the moment the interconnection with strategic partners, it is essentially an organization-wide client-server network with universal access. At one end is a vast data base, geographically scattered on multiple systems and replication servers. At the other end is the individual salesperson, continuously linked to this data base via a portable multimedia computer. From the salesperson's perspective, this giant network is entirely at his or her service, and the personal computer is the access port through which all requests will be made and answered.

There's our answer. In an Informed Sales Force, this information network must have three distinct tasks. First, to provide the salesperson with the information (product, customer, market) information he or she needs to competently deliver the factual side of the sales presentation. Second, to provide the materials to deliver a compelling, customized story that helps the salesperson enlist the customer's desire. Third, to deliver that information and story to the salesperson in the field, so that he or she can build the relationship by spending more time with the customer.

The mistake many companies make is to assume that the first two tasks are the same. Even companies whose marketing shows they know better—for example, they produce both dreamy theme ads and hard-nosed data sheets—often still arm their salespeople with one-size-fits-all sales materials thinly "customized" with the client's logo on the cover sheet.

The good news is that many companies are starting to get it right:

• At Gillette, the company's 250 reps are equipped with pen-based computers to help them service tens of thousands of small, individual retailers who sell shaving and personal care products. The system is still comparatively primitive, but it does enable the sales force to work almost continuously in the field. A Gillette rep can now sit down with a chain-store buyer and tell him, down to the individual store, which Gillette products are selling. As Tim Mathes, a Gillette regional sales manager, told *Sales & Marketing Management,* "It's almost impossible to put a value on what benefit we provide retailers as well as the benefit we get from being more focused."[7]

• Deere Power Systems, a division of John Deere Co. that makes diesel engines and other heavy equipment, discovered that its salespeople were often spending as much as a day digging through computer files for information relevant to an impending customer call. Then, after the call, they went back to the office and spent another day filling out forms and updating computer files.[8]

These delays, "caused gaps in the sales process and allowed competitors to beat us to a deal." The answer, at Deere Power, was to interlink the various data bases and then devote them to the individual salesperson, rather than the other way around. "We're trying to empower the salesperson with the collective intelligence of the organization," says Roger L. Pigg, manager of sales automation at the division.[9]

• Jack Butler, president of Butler Graphics in Troy, Michigan, pitches his service for automating the creation of newsletters and bulletins, using a desktop presentation that includes images, moving charts, and background music—

all customized to the potential client. One such presentation, to the automobile club AAA, resulted, Butler says, in "a $200,000 order on the spot."[10]

• At Perkin-Elmer Corp., the company's more than 200 North American sales reps use color laptops to help stay on top of its complex product catalog. For example, the firm's infrared instrument line comes in 2,000 different configurations. "It's really tough to keep up with what widgets go with which," says Michael H. Elliott, manager of sales and marketing systems.[11]

• Frustrated by falling productivity and annoyed customers, Compaq Computer did just the opposite of what was expected: it slashed its sales force almost in half, shut down three of its eight regional offices and sent the salespeople home. But it also armed those salespeople that remained with the company's own laptop computers, which were in turn supported by a giant (38 gigabyte) client-server information network that resided in each of the company's departments and held everything from press releases to technical reports to presentation graphics. The result, in a period when computer prices fell 50 percent, was a 30 percent increase in Compaq sales. Not surprisingly, many of these sales were to corporations wanting to duplicate Compaq's sales information system.[12]

• Baked goods are usually an impulse buy—and that plays havoc with the planning of baking companies, which never really know how much to produce or deliver on a given day. That was precisely the dilemma facing the $450 million Metz Baking Co. of Sioux City, Iowa. The company's 1,400 sales reps typically delivered bread, fruitcakes, and tarts to 40,000 grocery stores, delis, and restaurants each day. According to Larry Hames, the company's MIS vice president, the reps:

> would make their best guess of what they needed over their entire route over the next week; we'd bake that amount of product, roughly divided by day; and they'd attempt to sell it on a daily basis. If you ended up short by the end of your route, one of your accounts would have to do without. Or you might end up dumping all your excess product at the last stop.[13]

The solution Hames hit upon was palmtop computers, and in 1991 at a cost to the company of $7.5 million, all 1,400 reps were equipped with one. Now, each morning at one of Metz's 250 distribution centers, reps pick up their palmtops (downloaded overnight with demand information they gained the day before), check their inventories and start their rounds. At each stop, stale goods are removed and listed in the computer and fresh replacements put on the shelf. Says Hames, "Now our drivers can track demand on a daily basis by account. No more ballpark figures."[14] But, just as important, by not running short or dumping excess goods and by always keeping retailers' shelves fully stocked with fresh goods, Metz perpetually makes the best possible presentation to its customers.

• In what may be the ultimate test of technology in action, the chaos of trade shows, Andrew Corporation of Orland Park, Illinois, a marketer of transmission antenna towers, has armed its salespeople with notebook computers. Now when a potential customer enters the Andrew booth and asks for a quote or proposal, a salesperson can instantly contact headquarters—even the visitor's office—and generate on the spot the requested documents. "Our customers are dazzled by the speed at which we help them," Bobbi Rick, company exhibit manager, told *Sales & Marketing Management.*

VIRTUAL SELLING

What these examples show is that many progressive companies have made the crucial step of linking the corporate information system to the sales process. In doing so, the actual contact between the salesperson and the potential customer is transformed. Now it is no longer the customer relating to the individual sales rep, but, figuratively, to the knowledge and capabilities of that rep's entire company. Unquestionably this is a richer, more secure, and more appealing opportunity—and one more likely to lead to a sale.

The term is *virtual selling,* a variant on "virtual corporation."[15] If Total Sales Quality is our philosophy and an Informed Sales Force is our goal, then it follows that Virtual Selling, the infusion of the corporate information network into the actual moment of selling, is the underlying process.

Virtual Selling is the application of information technology to bring all of the company's resources and capabilities to bear to provide the customer with a complete solution to his unique requirements.

One of these resources is the salesperson himself, and it is the task of that salesperson to act as the intermediary between the customer and the corporate information network. It also follows from this definition that:

Virtual Selling

• Field sales and telesales become increasingly congruent, differing only in whether the salesperson is physically present or geographically distant as he or she electronically delivers the presentation.

• The presentation phase of the sale is no longer the art of drawing the customer towards the product, but enlisting that customer into product definition.

• Marketing gains the new task of using the presentation phase not only to tell the story, but also becomes an apparatus for learning about the potential customer in order to prepare for a long-term relationship.

• Corporate operations like advertising, public relations, human resources, publications, and graphic design, that until now have been only marginally connected to the sales process, now become heavily linked to it.

Ultimately, virtual selling may even take on the characteristics of virtual reality. It is not hard to imagine a salesperson and customer, a thousand miles apart but together in hyperspace, putting various product configurations through their paces—all before a single model is ever built. This is already taking place in architecture, where architects, equipped with a workstation and Autodesk software, regularly take clients on "walks" through a 3-D image of a proposed building design.

The kinds of presentations demanded by something like virtual selling will be as much an art form as a vehicle for information conveyance. It will mean integrating the sophistication of television commercials with the scope of corporate parts catalogs and the human interface of an expert systems program. Those capabilities in turn will demand animation, 3-D modeling, audio, speech synthesis, color graphics, full-motion video, software agents, desktop publishing, presentational tools geared for large quantities of data, data-entry interfaces and applications yet to be discovered.

The hardware and software infrastructure demanded by these applications has already been described in Chapter 5. But that alone will not be enough. The content of these presentational tools will have to be created and re-created. This is beyond the abilities of salespeople, nor should they be asked to devote the time to do so. On the contrary, the whole point of Total Sales Quality is to free the sales force to make sales, not waste hours creating videos. The contribution of the sales force in this process should be limited to customizing the tools to the individual customer's requirements.

Who then will make these presentations? The company already employs people with precisely such skills. They work in marketing communications. If we subscribe to our definition of virtual selling, then these resources need to be at least partially redirected away from the external activities of the company (placing ads and stories) and towards the internal activity of developing presentation (and, at the same time, information-gathering) tools for sales. As it happens, this shift of marketing communications from the mass media to more customer-directed activities is exactly what has been predicted by theorists of the new corporation.

Looking at the case studies described earlier in this chapter, it is apparent that each is slowly groping toward this ultimate sales presentation model. Yet, as innovative and potent as each of these programs is, one cannot also help noting that in a fundamental and vital way each is deeply flawed. To understand why, we need to return to our two sales personality types: the charmer and the techie.

The beginning Virtual Selling programs put in place by each of these companies seem to fall neatly into one category or another. Thus, Waters Chromatography is a charmer system, while Metz Bakery is a techie. There is nothing wrong with this, as the happy results enjoyed by both firms attest. But, ultimately the goal must be to amplify the strengths of each member of a company's sales force and supplement the weaknesses. A charmer presentation program may help the techies in the sales force beef up their relationship-building with customers, but it does little to complement the weaknesses of the charmers or make them more credible to customers. The reverse is just as true.

This imbalance is an inherent danger in trying to implement a virtual sales program without a guiding principle like Total Sales Quality. The best solution is one that balances pitch with content, story-telling with hard data. And the best way to assure that this happens is to enlist *all* of the company's operations into the selling process, and to guarantee universal access to information.

SOLVING THE PROBLEM

In retrospect, one of the most telling features of the traditional model of face-to-face selling is how unintegrated it is. First, you identify a qualified prospect. Then you make the pitch, which is often deliberately tangential and only remotely connected to the sale itself. This is the story-telling phase, and once you detect certain signals from the potential customer you quickly switch out of this mode and into the configuration mode. This second interval is relatively brief because traditionally there aren't that many options. ("We got it in any color you want, as long as it is black.") Then, once you've roughly determined the customer's taste (and psychologically gotten them to make their first commitment) you then launch into a programmatic close.

What most sales automation tools accomplish is to accentuate your ability to perform the first three tasks. The underlying model remains essentially intact.

But if we look at the same process through the lens of virtual selling, odd things begin to happen. In particular, the walls between the steps begin to disappear.

Consider the case of 3M Telecom Systems. In 1994, this 3M division announced that it would be conducting field trials of new multimedia software for its sales force's laptop computers.[16] This software would manage on-board CD-ROM drives in the laptops which would contain the catalogs, product data sheet, and promotional materials covering all of the company's 750 products and many times that number of accessories. According to James Diaz, the company's international marketing services manager, the system "will contain text and photos plus animation sequences that show how products work."[17]

Now imagine you are a 3M Telecom salesperson using one of these laptops on a customer visit. You open up the computer and launch into a presentation. You are showing colorful promotion graphics, demonstrating products and pulling up spec sheets into windows on the computer screen. With perhaps twenty thousand different product combinations, how do you know what to talk about? *You ask the customer.* What are your current needs? Are there any special performance requirements? How about accessories? Do have a budget for this purchase? The answers you get tell you what presentation tools to draw up next. Notice that in pulling up both catalog and promotional materials you are covering both sides of the charmer/techie coin.

But also notice something else: *The presentation IS the configuration.* By the time you've interactively customized your pitch to the prospective customer's needs, you've also managed not only to gather reams of knowledge about the customer that will be useful in the future, but also designed the product that the customer wants. More precisely, both of you have done the designing—thus, your customer, by joining in the presentation, finds himself or herself two-thirds of the way through the entire sales process.

One interesting side effect of Virtual Selling is that it not only focuses the process down upon the most appropriate configuration of a particular product for a customer . . . but, when that pathway proves unacceptable (because the company doesn't make that product configuration, the customer doesn't really know what he or she wants, etc.), it also allows you to smoothly change directions. For example, at Hewlett-Packard, Jim Kucharczyk, the national manager of sales programs for computer products, says, "The best compliment I've received is that this system eliminates the 'I'll get back to you' syndrome. Deals are closed on the spot because, if the customer inquires about another product, the rep has been able to pull up the necessary data [on the computer], rather than leave and return with another three-ring binder."[18]

THE DEATH OF THE CLOSE

Actually, more than two-thirds . . .

If the presentation process largely subsumes the configuration step, the two together destroy the need for the old-fashioned close. In other words, *in virtual selling the presentation, configuration, and close are the same thing.* So, virtual selling not only integrates the two types of information flowing from the company to the salesperson, but it also integrates the sales process itself into a nearly seamless whole.

This is a long way from the old way of wrapping up a sale. Closing a sale has, understandably, been an obsession of the sales profession for generations. Numerous books have been written, and untold seminars held, on the topic. After all, if you can't get that near-customer to affix signature to contract, all of your time and effort has been wasted.

Not surprisingly, this obsession has turned into dogma, complete with its own liturgy. As most readers will know, there is a whole collection of established closing techniques. They even have names. There's the Ben Franklin, with its competing lists of customer likes and dislikes. There's the Trial Close, which continuously plumbs the customer's attitudes towards various purchase scenarios. And there's the almost surreal Assumptive Close, in which the salesperson ignores all evidence to the contrary and blithely behaves as if the sale is already a *fait accompli*. Sales managers are constantly reminding their people of the ABC's: "Always Be Closing." Historically, "the close" has been a process of attempting to convince the customer to buy a product or service that only marginally meets the customer's requirements and which the customer does not thoroughly understand.

There is a touch of absurdity to all this, especially since a growing number of people on the receiving end of these closes know them too. Because Sales-Force-Automation tools usually only address the first two steps, they force even those salesmen with $10,000 laptop computers in their hands to still shift into the old hustle to close.

But Virtual Selling is different. Go back to our salesperson sitting in the customer's office using the computer to make a multimedia presentation. As we've already said, by the time the presentation is completed, the product has not only been configured for the customer, but by the customer. That customer is now looking at a product which, by the process itself, is as close as the customer can get to providing what he or she wants and needs.

At this point, there is really only one more step—and that is to find out when the company can create that product or service. Hence the need by the salesperson for real-time access to the factory. Query to manufacturing: can you build this order and deliver it in two weeks?

If the answer is affirmative and the delivery time is within the customer's requirements, there is only a single question left: *Do you want it?* And many times that won't even be necessary. The contract will already be automatically configured and can be quickly printed out for signing. The order is then transmitted in.

We have brought information technology to bear to identify a valid prospect and, most importantly, to develop a thorough understanding of the customer's requirement and to deliver a perfectly tailored, unique solution to that customer's requirements. The virtual sale. The virtual close.

Will it always succeed? No, there will always be people who shy away at the last moment. But can you have any doubt that the likelihood of a successful sale (and a happy subsequent business relationship) with this method, with the customer this deeply involved in the process, will be much more likely than with the old bag of tricks?

Of course, some people will always be more successful at selling than others. Great salespeople will likely still be great salespeople, though their productivity will still see an improvement. The real change will occur to everyone else: the good salesperson has a chance to become a great one because the technology will compensate for certain skill weaknesses; and the mediocre, or even bad, salesperson will be buoyed up by the tools to a level of performance far beyond anything possible before. Thus, though the talents of a given sales force may still be a bell-shaped curve, the median of that curve will shift towards higher productivity—and the company will be the beneficiary.

The biggest reason for this upward shift in productivity is that virtual selling improves the odds with every repeat visit. Whereas with the traditional techniques you may return to find a wary customer, embittered by a gnawing sense of being snookered, now you come back incrementally better equipped to improve what was a positive experience in the first place.

Based upon the information you gathered during previous contacts, you now have a solid foundation of knowledge about that customer from which to work. For example, you've learned that that customer only buys white sedans with air conditioning, so you don't waste your time (or the customer's patience) trying to flog a black convertible.

Since you already know the customer's tastes and desires you now can come prepared with a working solution and quickly gather any new updated information, describe recent new products or focus on any nuances of the order that might increase the customer's satisfaction. The sales process becomes more and more painless, until, the customer personally manages the whole process in what is the ultimate guarantee of customer satisfaction.

With your help, the customer has become more knowledgeable, more *informed*—and more capable of determining his or her own solutions using your products. This too is a closure:

> The goal of Virtual Selling is a Total Quality Sale to an Informed Customer.

The circle of mutually beneficial and trusting business relationships, linking manufacturer to the supply chain, to the distribution channel and now, at last, to the customer, is finally complete.

Chapter 9

Rethinking Sales Management

J ust about every word in this book so far has been dedicated to the individual salesman and saleswoman and how the organization must reorient and revise itself to serve them ... and through them, the customer. Almost nothing has been said about sales management.

By this point the reader would be justified in asking why sales management should even be discussed. After all, with an Informed Sales Force of empowered salespeople conducting virtual selling backed by a massive corporate information infrastructure, aren't traditional sales managers now obsolete? Haven't they been rendered as superfluous as all those other middle managers we read about being laid off as corporations restructure and flatten out?

Actually, *no*. In the world of Virtual Selling, sales managers remain as vital as ever. The difference is—as with all those other corporate middle managers that are still around—that their role changes so radically that many of the traits for which they were rewarded in the past will now become a mark of incompetence, while many characteristics once regarded (and punished) as weakness will now prove to be strengths.

This role reversal in turn suggests that sales management will experience as great a trauma and future shock as any job in the modern organization. It also hints that many currently successful sales managers—from district and regional sales managers all the way up to vice presidents of sales—will find themselves suddenly not up to the job and struggling to keep their careers alive. Meanwhile, other individuals, some of whom now haven't the least interest in sales, will be amazed to find themselves not only in sales management, but thriving.

Once again, this sounds like all the ingredients for a massive dislocation at the best, most visionary companies, and a disaster for those shortsighted companies that are caught unawares. And, once again, to understand how we got into this predicament, we need to look back at the history of sales management and see how the recent arrival of technology and automation have sent it off on the wrong trajectory.

MANAGING STRUGGLE

The traditional sales manager, the one we know so well, is an unlikely combination of high-school football coach, Santa Claus, and hanging judge. Typically a former star salesman, his paradoxical task is to take a diverse group of individual salespeople and form them into a cohesive team with a common mission—while at the same time induce a life-or-death struggle amongst that team's members. This contradiction defines the sales manager's two daily tasks:

1. Act as a cheerleader and morale-builder to maintain the salespeople's loyalty to the company and to spur them on to greater productivity and performance.
2. Dispense rewards (bonuses, prizes, better territories and promotions) to over-achievers and punishments (lousier territories, weaker leads, and even termination) to under-achievers.

These two tasks inevitably define the organization of the sales office. In order to perform the cheerleading job, the traditional sales manager must bring the salespeople together on a regular basis. These regular gatherings also serve as the platform for the public dispensation of rewards and punishments. Fairly determining who gets what requires keeping tabs not only on the actual sales closed by the salespeople, but also their efforts. This in turn means extensive records and forms filled out daily by each salesperson listing his itinerary, calls, contacts, status, expected close date, etc.

In this traditional model, the marginal amount of training occurs in two ways: either at the annual company sales meeting, where an endless stream of product development people from headquarters march through quick slide shows and hand out binders of data sheets to take home; or *ad hoc*, through an unofficial guild system by which long-tenured veteran salespeople take newly arrived apprentices out on calls and teach them to perform demos.

The strengths and weaknesses of this sales management model are part of American myth. And it is important to remember that, for all the things wrong with this model, it worked well for a century. Why? Ironically, because of its limitations. For all of the oppressive features of the system back at the sales office, once the salesman walked out the door he was essentially a free entrepreneur, constructing his day and his sales methodology as he went along. By the same token, the star system, for all of its abuses, did recognize the limitations of the existing information system (limited qualification of leads, inadequate documentation, poor training) and moved towards maximum efficiency by empowering certain individuals to make their own decisions and then arming them with the most likely prospects to close. It was sloppy, but, in all, probably the best alternative.

The arrival of automation did to sales management pretty much what it did to sales itself: it produced an initial productivity increase at the cost of amplifying all of the old model's flaws. For example, the sales meeting/guild model for training wasn't replaced; instead, salespeople still learned from office veterans, but now at the annual sales meetings they saw color overheads and were sent home with twice as many binders of unreadable product information. Meanwhile, as a 15-year study by the VASS Co. ending in 1994 concluded, "Seventy percent of managers believe that selling—the highest paid profession in our culture—can be learned without training."[1]

The cheerleading didn't end either: now entire Mondays could be spent watching corporate television and videos, and salespeople not only could fight to the death to make

Rethinking Sales Management

quotas with their office peers, but with every company salesperson around the world.

But the most visible effect of automation was on management's ability to gather information on its sales staff. If the traditional salesman was free the moment he hit the street, the automated salesman or saleswoman became electronically tethered to management almost every second of the day. In telesales, computers could now track every single call made by a salesperson during the day, measure its duration, even regularly tap in to see if the right words were being said or if superfluous human conversation was slowing performance. Meanwhile, in the field, the arrival of laptop computers proved an invitation for even more reporting. Now every transaction with the home office could be tracked, and, by headquarters fiat, all customer contacts would be punched in and conveyed to management.

In keeping with the nomenclature used earlier, you might call this automation model *computer-integrated sales management*, or, as embittered salespeople know it, *Big Brother*. Like most such nicknames, this one is dead on: there is something totalitarian and Orwellian about management going to such great pains to keep tabs on every minute of the working lives of its individual salespeople. And, like all the other top-down, open-ended automation techniques we've looked at, this model causes more damage than it repairs.

Yet, while the growing frustration among salespeople with the Big Brother model has received considerable attention, what has gone unremarked is that the putative "winners" in this model, sales managers, are actually victims too. The digitization of sales essentially reduces the sales manager to the role of highly-paid clerk, a passive conduit conveying endless minutiae from the field up to Big Brother and then, in turn, passing the supposedly "objective" rewards and punishments based on that data back down to the field.

In this model, if sales is oppressed, sales management is gutted. And, to carry the scenario to its ultimate conclusion: if sales management is impotent, why do you need it at all? A cynic might suggest that it only survives in many companies to insulate (and take the blame for) top management from a dispirited and angry sales force.

This situation clearly cannot last.

But that brings us back to where we began this chapter. If the Virtual Selling model turns the organization upside down, and Total Sales Quality essentially reverses the flow of information, isn't sales management still caught in the limbo of the middle?

Not necessarily. The mistake is to assume it is the modern automated model that is getting flipped, not the traditional one. In the traditional model, sales management had a very distinct role: it was the home office's liaison to the field. Now it becomes more clear:

In Virtual Selling, sales management is the field's liaison with the home office.

But what does that mean? Three tasks come immediately to mind: advocate, tool-maker, and organizer.

SALES ADVOCATE

In Virtual Selling, sales management represents the sales force to the rest of the company and acts as its advocate.

Rethinking Sales Management

Why? One reason is that the whole purpose of this new model is to keep sales focused on the job at hand, *selling*. Moreover, during the establishment of the new sales organization, and during its maturation thereafter, its needs must be represented before the larger enterprise. Someone must serve as sales' surrogate and advocate at headquarters. This task naturally falls on sales management because it alone understands the needs of both parties.

Hasn't this always been sales management's job? Yes, but in the past such advocacy has been largely circumstantial or anecdotal, a good manager going to bat for a valued employee. In the main, most sales managers have accepted the alternate role, that of being the instrument of top management policy. That will no longer be acceptable.

The biggest advocacy challenges most sales managers will now face is convincing the company to design its IS system to support Total Sales Quality, in investing in the hardware and software that will drive the sales information wing of this system, and finally, in equipping the sales force with the equipment it needs to access this system. If sales management can succeed at this, other goals, such as TSQ, sales force empowerment, virtual selling—and ultimately, an Informed Sales Force—will almost inevitably follow.

Some sales managers already realize this: in the words of Charlie Causey, southeastern regional sales manager for Owens-Corning's insulation division, "As spans of control increase, sales people automatically become more empowered. They become real managers of their own business and their own territories."[2]

But without an initial defining success, the larger goals become almost impossible.

But is sales management, with its limited knowledge of technology up to the job? It has no choice. It cannot pass off the task to other, more qualified, corporate departments because, simply, they cannot be trusted. In 1993, in listing "The 10 Biggest Mistakes of SFA", *Sales & Marketing Management* gave prominent placement to "Overlooking the People," "Ducking the Big Brother Issue" and "Uncontrolled Departmental Rivalries"—all three likely results of trusting the construction of the sales information system to nonsales departments. Wrote the magazine:

> . . . Dominant members—either forceful individuals or groups that have strong political clout in the company—will try to push the system design in a direction that supports their specific needs.
>
> For example, senior managers might see the system as a way to establish greater control over sales people, but MIS envisions it as a rich new source of data. Engineering and production groups, on the other hand, view it as a product design or field service tool. The marketing department sees it as a strategic weapon. The sales department considers it a tactical tool.
>
> Who is right? In a way, everyone. The problem is, if you let one of these groups dominate the process and force its agenda on everyone else, your system will ultimately fail.
>
> Most likely, the sharpest conflicts will be between MIS and sales. Since salespeople are generally results-oriented, opportunistic, intuitive and relatively unstructured in their approach to individual tasks, they're bound to clash with MIS people, who tend to prefer a structured, logical and disciplined approach to problem solving.[3]

There is only one group in a corporation that understands both the long-term needs of the company and the
short-term desires of the sales force, and it sits athwart the
communications path between MIS and the field: sales
management.

But in accepting that job, sales management also assumes
some new responsibilities. One of these, suggested above,
is that sales managers—and not just vice presidents, but all
the way down to district managers—must break from their
usual tactical view of the task to a more strategic attitude
that incorporates the long-term needs of the organization.
That new viewpoint will be vital if sales is to convince the
rest of the company that this re-engineering (and apparent
loss of power by other departments) is really to everyone's
advantage.

In other words, sales is going to have to sell itself within
the organization. And, as with any other kind of selling,
sales is going to have to prove to the rest of the company
that its product, itself, is superior in performance and benefits to the company to any other contender for the job—be
it MIS, marketing, manufacturing, even Executive Row.
Working to sales' advantage is precisely that it knows how
to pitch, sell and close better than anybody else in the organization. But to its disadvantage, sales prides itself on being
a maverick, an outsider and of divided loyalties—hardly
virtues to recommend it for the job as the ultimate corporate insider.

What all of this suggests is that if sales is to take its place
as the new focal point of a company dedicating itself to
Total Sales Quality, then it must prove itself worthy of the
job. And to do that, the sales department must begin by

transforming itself first, with or without corporate support.

TOOLMAKER

In Virtual Selling, sales management assures, through new tools and processes, that the sales force is fully equipped to conduct Virtual Selling and fully served to achieve Total Sales Quality.

The second task of sales management deals with the mechanism of selling itself. It is one thing to announce Virtual Selling and Total Sales Quality, it is another thing to implement them. Some party in the organization needs to identify what tools the individual salesperson needs to conduct point-of-sale promotions, contract development, and competently tap into the vast information infrastructure designed to help complete a sale. That means intelligently picking out hardware and software, the latter including not only off-the-shelf programs, but also determining what new tools need to be custom-designed. And this should be a continuing, not a one time only, process.

A perfect example of this new point of view can be found in the words of Bob Boylard, Causey's boss and vice president of sales for Owens-Corning's insulation division:

My number-one priority is to get information out of my people, to quit being the keeper of the keys [at company headquarters] in Toledo, and let our salespeople be keepers of their own keys. If I can't empower my salespeople, then I'm not going to be able to move very far along this technology highway that seems to be offering us such tremendous opportunities.[4]

Such a responsibility cannot be placed upon the sales force itself for obvious reasons. Most salespeople aren't technologists—some, after their experiences with automation to date, are actively anti-technology—so they would likely have little idea of either what's available or what's possible. Furthermore, being essentially entrepreneurs, the system that salespeople would envision probably would not have the needs of the corporation in mind.

Nor can tool creation be placed in the hands of other corporate departments. Again, this risks results that reward those departments and not sales. So, in the end, as with advocacy, tool making comes down to sales management as the only group with the right balance of detachment and interest.

Here's an example of why only sales management can properly do this job: every sales manager knows, but few nonsales types understand, that there are three basic ways to structure a sales force. According to marketing and sales consultant Frank Lynn, these three types can be defined as:

1. *Project-structured:* transitory sales forces that come together on a project-by-project basis, such as targeting a new market niche.
2. *Product-structured:* usually found in small and medium-sized companies and organized around a single product line.
3. *Account-structured:* the opposite of the product-structured force, this type (also known as a "pooled sales force") is organized to support a particular customer.[5]

Does manufacturing, even marketing, understand the philosophical differences between the three? The different kind of information they need to succeed? How the potential personality clashes in each demand a different kind of management?

And that is only the start. What the most forward-looking sales theoreticians are beginning to understand is that companies in the future won't reorganize sales along these types every few months, but *continuously*, structuring and restructuring *ad hoc* organizations daily, hourly, as the need presents itself.

Creating that kind of fluid, adaptable sales structure will require the most sophisticated forms of workteam software ("groupware"), broadband communications networks, and innovative new forms of management. This will be hard enough for experienced sales managers to understand and put in place; it would seem impossible for anyone else in the organization.

But assuming such work will place some heavy demands on sales management. In particular, to select or develop the equipment and tools needed by Virtual Selling, the sales manager must first develop his or her own expertise in information technology. Management will no longer be the place where you hide from laptop computers, fax-modems and productivity software, but at the head of the march towards them.

When asked what sales managers should do to prepare themselves for this future, marketing guru Don Schultz replied, "If you want to go back and get some education, get it in data bases, basic research, and market information. And you need to learn more about logistics than in the past."[6]

The sales manager of an Informed Sales Force will not have to be a programmer or a systems analyst, but should at least understand the capabilities of this and the next generation of laptop computers, know the operation of the best available sales software (as well as the most commonly used business programs), be proficient with on-line services and telecommunications and be a master of the company's own data bases with info-grid. He or she should also have developed a relationship with a good programmer and helped develop a couple of specialized tools and presentations for his or her salespeople—and soon, when user-friendly object-oriented programming tools are available, create one of this new type of program.

SALES FORCE ORGANIZER

In Virtual Selling, sales management organizes corporate resources and applies its own talents to help the sales force work at its maximum productivity.

Even with a corporate-wide, TSQ-oriented information infrastructure in place, and even with the sales force armed with the hardware and software it needs to conduct virtual selling, we are still not all the way to the Informed Sales Force. The reason is that sales forces and the companies they serve are not static monoliths, but ever-changing human institutions. There will still be angry customers, unhealthy competition between employees, power-grabbing, and a wide range of talents and aptitudes. There will also still be sudden and unexpected market shifts, economic spikes and downturns, and unfaithful or crooked customers. Total Sales Quality can only minimize the effect of these forces, it cannot stop them.

Therefore, once the information system is in place and the sales force fully equipped, the job sales management isn't over. For one thing, it will still have to advocate for improvements in the infrastructure as new technologies come on the scene, and it will have to develop new tools and processes to take advantage of those advances. By the same token, sales management will always have to be vigilant against encroachments on the role of sales, because ambition is part of a successful organization.

But there is more. In our lifetime at least, no technological system, no matter how powerful, will be able to conduct all of the training required of new sales reps, or even the skill tune-ups of veteran salespeople. Nor will any system be able to fully identify a weakness in a salesperson's selling skills and help fill that gap. Nor will it advocate unusual secondary skills—golf, perhaps, or wine connoisseurship—that might make the difference in closing a sale.

The information system will not have intuition or the kind of hunches that come from a lifetime in sales. It will not be able to identify that a salesperson has personal problems that are affecting his or her performance. It will not know when people need to blow off steam; when they need their spirits lifted; or when their morale needs a boost. But most of all, no system will be able to bring to a compensation system anything more than a purely empirical measure. Only an experienced manager, now armed with greater information than ever about such elusive factors as customer satisfaction and relationship development, as well as a gut sense about a salesperson's potential, can arrive at a truer and fairer compensation.

There is also a big challenge looming that arises from all of this independence given to sales. By making the individual salesperson more entrepreneurial and self-contained, this model also weakens that salesperson's links to the parent company. This will be happening everywhere in the company, and as some business theorists have suggested, this will shift the role of all corporate operations towards a greater focus on internal communications, employee identity building, and morale.[7] But the task will fall particularly hard upon sales management, where the ties are loose to begin with. The solutions sales management will find will vary with the company, but it is likely to include daily e-mail, newsletters, new award programs, and regular social gatherings.

Says Jim Kucharczyk of HP: ". . . nothing replaces pressing the flesh. When we do get together [in regional meetings], we make sure a significant portion of time is dedicated to formal or informal team-building exercises. Maybe we'll have dinner together, or go bowling."[8]

Helping this loyalty building, Kucharczyk adds, is the increased satisfaction of the salespeople themselves in their jobs, "their appreciation of the investment we made in them. It's also motivational for them to know that we're letting them do what they want to do, which is to spend more of their time in front of their customers."[9]

This is the old cheerleading transformed into something more subtle; not just temporary ego-boosting, but helping the individual salesperson become more productive, more competent and more satisfied—and more loyal to the organization. Says Don Schultz:

> So there will be a different kind of sales manager, who is not just the traditional get-'em-jazzed-up, go-out-and-make-the-goals type. The sales manager is going to be much more involved as a *manager of resources*, not only the sales resource and sales people, but helping to manage the resources in the organization.[10]

In theory, sales managers are supposed to be doing this now. But in every way, the system works against it. The top-down management style of most organizations typically makes sales management the enemy of the sales force, a situation hardly conducive to the kind of trust needed for the personal relationships we're talking about.

And even if that trust was there, the current information structure, with its endless demand for more and more reams of data from the field and from sales management, leaves little time for the personal touch.

RETURN TO LEADERSHIP

There is no escaping the fact that the transition to a Total Sales Quality model will be rough on sales management. The increased spans of control made possible by technology and sales force empowerment will inevitably reduce the need for as many managers. Some will find a place back in sales . . . and find themselves thrilled to land in this new world of Virtual Selling and career independence. But others will have to move on.

Rethinking Sales Management

The most likely to be affected by the shift will be those managers whose personality traits made them uniquely suited to the older models. Autocratic but charismatic, manipulative but quick-thinking managers thrived in the traditional model, but their controlling style will defeat them when dealing with Virtual Selling. Decisively bureaucratic and numbers-first managers were amply rewarded in the sales automation world, but their lack of contact with their sales reps and their even greater lack of flexibility will often find them without the important subjective leadership skills required under the new model.

Meanwhile, a new type of sales manager will rise to the fore. He or she will exhibit an interesting new combination of techie and natural leader—a pairing of traits until now rarely found in sales managers but, curiously, in legendary business executives like Gates, Noyce, Packard, and Watson. This can only bode well.

Of course, that is little consolation to professionals who, after decades of building a career in the Old Regime, now find themselves in the middle of a revolution. To them, there is only one consolation: no one ever goes into management to become a glorified file clerk. You go there because you have a talent for leading people, for organizing them and for helping them achieve more than they thought possible. But automation has all but evaporated that purpose. And the future looks even more bleak: more data, more reports, less time to be a manager. Total Sales Quality and Virtual Selling do just the opposite—the more efficient they become, the more "Informed" the sales force, the more you, as a manager, are freed to bring to bear the value-added people skills you do best.

This is our final convergence. At its intersection the dream of every sales manager will come true: management, at last, will be synonymous with leadership.

Chapter 10

The Informed Sales Force

*You can design the best process in the world, and back it with
the latest and greatest technology; but if your people don't
buy into the project, it won't work. . . . The most successful
[sales information] programs are those where the vision and
benefits are shared across the organization from day one.*
—Insight Technology Group Report, April 1995

L et's take a look at Virtual Selling at work. This is how
it can be, as the following scenario, concerning a man
named Andy, indicates:

It is seven A.M. on a warm July morning. The kids are in the
den watching the last bit of TV before they leave for summer
school. Andy's wife, in her suit, is in the kitchen, making bag
lunches before she leaves for the office. The dog is pacing by
the front door, waiting to be let out.

221

Andy, still in his bathrobe and carrying a mug of coffee, tucks the newspaper and his notebook computer under his arm and shuffles out to the back patio. Gonna be a beautiful day, he decides.

Sitting down at the patio table, Andy takes a slug of coffee and then turns on the computer. He types in his password, and then, as the machine uses its wireless modem to call in, Andy turns to look at the newspaper. He is hardly through the headlines, when his software agent—a blue square on the screen bearing the logo "Andrew Moeller's Assistant"—announces, "Good morning. We've received some items during the night. Do you wish to see them?"

Beats the tripe in the newspaper. Andy taps the return key. Up on the screen comes his company's daily newspaper, complete with stories, videos, classified ads, even an active bulletin board. Andy checks the latest news—he whistles at the announcement of Bob Trotter's sale to Volvo ("Maybe I ought to transfer to the Stockholm office," Andy says to himself), checks the stock price and saves a technical article for later reference—then moves on.

"Do you wish to see your schedule for the day?" asks the agent. Andy taps the key. Up comes the day's schedule, blocked out by the quarter hour.

First up, at ten A.M., is Protectron Corp. Andy smiles at the memory. Protectron. Carl West, director of procurement, the toughest buyer in town. Protectron is the hottest company in electronic home controllers—from an apartment to $2 billion in six years—so you couldn't ignore it. But dealing with West was like walking into a tree shredder. The man prided himself on his encyclopedic knowledge and his merciless interrogation skills. Some veteran salesmen and saleswomen had walked into West's office and staggered out an hour later—after a barrage of questions and charges about benchmarks, service contracts, options, availabilities, delivery dates, and pricing—with their egos shattered and their contracts torn in two.

Andy remembered that his knees had actually knocked on that first visit to Protectron. The guys back at the office had a bet going whether he'd even emerge from West's office alive. Andy remembered Larry Stills pointing at the new computer in Andy's hand—this was right after the new TSQ system had been installed—and laughing, saying, "Buddy, that thing may be small, but it's too big to have to eat."

West even looked like a firebreather: brush cut (and not the hip type), white short-sleeved shirt, square-toed shoes and a tie that must have been twenty years old. He was the kind of guy who could say hello and shake your hand, both in a millisecond, and be back in his chair glaring at you before you even knew what happened.

Andy remembered feeling like a stain on the office chair. "Well?" asked West in a way that made a question sound like a challenge to a fistfight. "I don't have much time."

"This won't take long, Mr. West," Andy had said. "I want to show you our new 64-bit microcontroller, the 911436. It's to be formally announced next week and . . ."

"Read about it in EDN," said West dismissively. "Doesn't look like much."

"It will when you learn more about it," said Andy. He tossed his laptop on the table (a nice casual touch, he'd used it ever since), popped up the screen and booted up. For an instant he thought about using the slick new multimedia presentation that advertising had sent out the week before, but shrewdly decided to pass. It would kill with most procurement managers; but Carl West wasn't like most procurement managers. Instead, he went straight to the data sheet. It popped up on the screen, with a window in the upper right showing the new chip floating in space, followed by moving images of a number of potential applications.

West glanced at the screen. "I know all this. Tell me about your DSP."

Andy slid the cursor to the entry "Digital Signal Processing" and tapped a key. Up came eight densely packed pages of detailed performance specifications. "Will this do?" Andy asked, suppressing a smile, "or would you like the circuit diagram?"

"This'll do," West muttered. He read for a few minutes. Finally, without looking up, he muttered, "Can I get a copy of this?"

"Sure," said Andy, pulling a portable printer out of his briefcase. He reached over and touched the print key on the computer. The printer, not plugged into anything, hummed in his hand, printing out the eight pages in less than a minute. "Here you go," said Andy, handing the sheets over.

West's eyes flickered for a moment, then recovered. "Even if you've got the specs, that doesn't mean they're real. And it doesn't mean you can deliver. I get sales guys coming in here all the time with phony stats and vaporware they can never deliver. It's one thing to print out a data sheet, it's another to build a real product and deliver it on time."

Don't get angry, Andy had told himself. He forced a smile. "Mr. West, if I didn't believe in my company or its products I

The Informed Sales Force

wouldn't be here. I am not interested in selling to you once and then disappearing. My goal is to develop a long-term business partnership with Protectron. And that is only going to happen if I give you what you want when you want it."

West made a disbelieving smirk; he'd heard all this relationship stuff before. Okay, pal, thought Andy, watch this.

He reached over and typed a command into the computer. It would take twenty seconds to load the file. "Now, Mr. West, if you would be interested, I'd be happy to share with you the results of our beta tests. As you can see [up came the file with perfect timing], the 911436—we code-named it Dragonfly in-house by the way—has proven itself in a number of applications to meet the specs we've assigned to it." Up on the screen came one test result after another. "However, I do note your . . . skepticism, and I'm happy to say that one of our beta's was willing to identify himself and talk about the product."

"Yeah?" said West, leaning forward. "Who?"

Up came a windowed movie of Samuel Eastman, director of product development at Medi-Sys Corp., the medical equipment giant. Eastman looked like an old football player, which only added to his eloquence. As he extolled the performance of the Dragonfly in a number of testbed applications, other windows popped up showing the empirical results of the Medi-Sys tests. They validated, even exceeded, all of Andy's claims.

Now West was interested. He read the data with great intensity—so great that West barely noticed Andy getting up from his chair, walking around to stand beside him and begin tapping keys on a small side window.

That's what Andy had hoped would happen. He wanted to make the next part appear seamless.

A memo had come down from corporate a week before requiring at least one senior manager in manufacturing be on call at all times to receive communications from the field. As he heard the computer's on-board modem click on and softly begin dialing, he silently prayed that manufacturing hadn't ignored the dictum from above—those fab guys were notorious for ignoring even desperate pleas from the field.

The line connected. Thank God. Andy turned to look at West, and found him watching the new little window. "Now Mr. West," said Andy, not giving him time to speak, "you asked about availability." He quickly typed in name and greetings. Pleasepleaseplease, he said to himself, let it be somebody important.

On the screen came the reply, "This is Raymond Norling. I'm currently at Fab Facility 4 in Phoenix." Bingo! The vice president himself! Andy had to restrain himself from throwing a fist in the air. "Mr. Norling, I'm here with Carl West of Protectron. He has some questions about the Dragonfly. May he speak directly with you?"

"Yes," came back Norling's typed words and he listed the phone number of the nearest video phone. Andy hung up and typed in the number. Out of the corner of his eye, he caught West staring at him respectfully. Outside of a few little start-ups where everybody was an executive, West had probably never talked to a manufacturing v.p. in his life—especially not one of a Fortune 500 company. Neither had Andy, but he wasn't going to tell.

Andy moved closer to West and adjusted the little camera on the top of the computer. As he did, a new window popped up in the middle of the screen. There was Raymond Norling, in suit and tie, looking just like he did in the annual report. "Hello," he said in a sober baritone.

"Mr. Norling, I'd like to introduce you to Mr. West."

"A pleasure to meet you, Mr. West. I've long been an admirer of Protectron, and, after what Andy's told me about you, I've looked forward to meeting you."

Andy! Like we're old buddies. Andy almost laughed. What's Norling doing running factories? He's a born salesman.

"Now, Mr. West," the face on the screen continued, "how can I help you?"

There was a surprising new note of respectfulness in West's voice. "Well sir, we're looking seriously at your new controller. But we want to make sure that you'll be able to deliver it when we need it and in the quantities we desire."

The two men watched Norling glance down for a moment, and heard the tapping of keys. Norling glanced up again. "Here Mr. West, I'm sending you [a new window filled with statistics appeared on the screen] my current data on production figures and delivery estimates. You now know everything I do—and I think you'll see that we can meet just about any order you give us."

"Yes, well, er, thank you, Mr. Norling," said West, "I won't take up any more of your time. I certainly appreciate you doing this."

"Oh, it's my pleasure, Mr. West," said Norling, without a trace of irony. "And, as I'm sure Andy will tell you, we are more than prepared to send over a team to help you design the 911436 into your new product for the maximum performance and efficiency. I look forward to talking with you again."

As Andy turned off the video phone, he secretly rolled his eyes: who would have ever thought it? Before the meeting was over, Andy used the computer one more time: to draw up a sample contract.

A $15 million sale. A design win in the hottest new consumer product on the market. And a ten-day trip to Europe for two. As 24 e-mails later confirmed, Andy was the toast of the company. He, of course, gave due credit to Ray Norling and the designers in the IS department and marketing.

That was three months ago. Since then there had been a curious increase in the use of notebook computers and the company's sales information system. As for Protectron, if he and West weren't exactly going on camping trips together, at least Andy noticed that West treated him better than he treated his own Protectron subordinates. And when reps from other divisions at Andy's company called they were met, if not with open arms, then at least not with the usual tar and feathers.

Andy downed his coffee. Then he called up all records of the last month regarding Protectron. The computer took about a minute, during which Andy checked the box scores in the sports section. "The file is complete," announced Andy's software agent. "Please note that there are three added notes attached to the file."

Hmm. Wonder what those are about? Andy searched through the records. They contained complete details of every contact made with Protectron by Andy's firm, including sales presentations, phone calls, service visits, design team visits. There had been nine sales visits, six by Andy and three by Bob Lichte over in DRAMs. Bob had even landed a small sale. Good for him. Also listed were files containing every sales presentation given to West, right back to the first one. There were also some spiffy multimedia presentations prepared by marcom that Andy had filed because they might be of future use. And there were copies of all past correspondence, e-mails (74 of them) and contracts.

Andy popped up the service records. Six of them. Not too bad. Uh-oh. One of the calls was red-tagged. That must be one of the notes. He opened the file and was immediately transferred to a week-old note [I've got to tell my agent to notify me of these things, Andy muttered to himself] from a Marie Neelson in support. It said that Protectron was growing frustrated by what it saw as shipping delays of the new 3.3-volt version of Dragonfly, especially as it threatened Protectron's own impending introduction of its new battery-powered handheld master home controller.

Neelson had shrewdly not only notified sales and marketing of the problem, but also sent word out through the company's entire communications network, from suppliers to customers. A gutsy call, but it had worked. Andy scrolled through the scores of replies, from everybody from the silicon wafer supplier (nothing they could do) all the way to a maker of automobile power seat motors in Lavonia, Michigan. As it happened, they had 25,000 extra 3.3-volt 911436's thanks to a reduced order from General Motors, and they'd be happy to send them back for credit.

Neatly done. Now the other two notes. This time good news. One was from Lichte, the other from a guy named Herb on the design time visiting Protectron. Both had the same message: Protectron was preparing a new generation of home controllers that would require faster access times, faster input/output and parallel processing. Might be a good opportunity. Herb had even sent along the preliminary specs for a new chip, the 911536 "Butterfly" that, linked in pairs from two to six, might just do the job.

Andy typed out short e-mails thanking everybody. Butterfly, eh? Let's try it. He tapped into marketing to see if there were any new presentational materials on the product. Sure enough, six minutes of special effects and dramatized applications. Why not? The new Carl West will take the time to watch. But let's not press our luck, Andy said to himself, and also called up every spec sheet and manual draft on Butterfly he could find.

That was going to take a few minutes, so Andy took his coffee cup into the kitchen, said good-by to the kids, walked his wife to the door, then went to take a shower.

As he was tying his tie, Andy realized to his amazement that he was actually looking forward to seeing Carl West. After all, it had been six weeks since they'd last met face to face. In the interim, of course, they'd talked on the videophone, and every few days Andy passed on any useful information to Protectron. Once, he'd even let West log on through him and directly access the company's files. That had been a bit unnerving, but it had worked out fine. West, unaccustomed to trusting, or being trusted by, anyone, seemed pleased.

It had been great, freeing Andy to focus on potential new customers, but now Andy wanted to sit across from West and do some real selling. Show him the old razzle-dazzle again. With a jaunty move, Andy tightened the knot on his tie and walked back out to the patio.

One hundred twenty six megabytes of new materials had been loaded onto the disk in Andy's computer. He checked the index. All there.

He checked his watch. Okay, what else? He called up the calendar. The red box of the software agent appeared, "Don't forget that you have a 2 P.M. with Quark Inc. today."

Oh, yeah, the color laser printer guys. Possibly a medium-sized account. Well, they'll definitely want to see all the fireworks. He called up his standard opening presentation on the company's entire microcontroller family, telling the computer to emphasize Dragonfly and to modify it for the name "Quark." He also called up a biography of his contact—resume, family names, anything publicly available—and stored it to look at during lunch.

"You have one hour to be at your first appointment," said the software agent. "Do you need directions to any of your appointments today?" Andy tapped the cursor on Quark. After a few seconds, up came a road map with a suggested route. Andy saved that for later too.

He started to pack up, then had a hunch. Tapping a key to open a window, he touched the words "Le Papillon" and heard a phone ring. It was answered by the maitre d'. Andy made a reservation for two at noon. Hanging up, he closed the computer. Well, he thought, let's see if Carl West likes *nouvelle cuisine.*

At four o'clock, Andy was driving on the beltway just ahead of the rush-hour traffic, heading towards a restaurant ten miles ahead. It had been as successful a day as it had been beautiful. Just blue skies and good news, Andy told himself, the kind of day you wish you could file away somewhere so you can pull it out on the bad days.

He made a few more calls to customers and contacts on the cellular phone, then called in to the sales information system and, using its speech recognition program, "talked" to his software agent. It was, as always, a little weird and stilted—but it got the job done. A couple of appointments entered on the calendar, some presentation files downloaded onto the computer on the seat beside him, and some simple notes on today's meetings in case anyone wanted to check them tonight. Tomorrow morning he'd flesh them out.

And he had a lot to talk about. Carl West—what a pussycat he turned out to be once you got past the torture and interrogation phase—had been a little testy about the low-voltage Dragonfly problem. But that was mostly bluff, because once Andy recited back to him chapter and verse about how the company had moved mountains to find those extra chips in Michigan, West's edge instantly faded.

After that, it was easy. West not only sat rapt through the entire multimedia presentation on Butterfly, but was actually enthusiastic about Herb's new multiprocessor model. He asked for a copy of the memo and any supporting documentation, then called in the product manager on the new project. Andy kept waiting for the other shoe to drop, for West and the product weenie to suddenly find some hole in the data and turn on him, but it never happened. On the contrary, when the product guy hesitated once about divulging some proprietary information on the new product—a home controller that actually learned from the residents and began to anticipate their behavior—West actually intervened and said, "Go ahead and tell Andy about it. I'll vouch for him." Andy almost fell off his chair.

Then at lunch West turned out to be some kind of wine connoisseur genius and they ended with the owner of the restaurant taking a tour of the wine cellar. They departed with West

The Informed Sales Force

slapping Andy on the back and telling him he'd be in touch next week about price and volume . . . then added, almost as an aside, that Protectron would like to begin installing a data interchange system with Andy's company. It's a request from the top, West added. Could Andy start the process?

It wasn't the wine that floated Andy out to his car.

The afternoon appointment was almost a joke. Quark was a little start-up with a big future. Maybe. Probably, if their new printer could do what they said at the retail price they were quoting. And these guys were real gear heads. Andy knew their type: about all he had to do for the presentation was turn on the computer. After that, as they sat there for a half-hour with their jaws open, he could actually get up and go out for coffee.

But Andy knew better. Guys like this were a killer to close. In the old days, they'd pound you with arcane questions and minutiae for visit after visit, just enjoying the technology for its own sake. Months could go by before you even had a hope of commitment—and they were just as likely to turn up low on cash and thank you for your trouble. Or they might prove to be the next Apple.

That was one of the glories of the new system. You could let these guys ask questions to the heart's content, until their brains melted, and you'd never run out of answers. Even better, you could turn the computer over to them and let them surf the system . . . while you sat back and watched them, learned from their reactions, determined who was the decision maker, and prepared yourself to push the deal to the next phase. No more being distracted by your own presentation. Now you could have fun and just focus on the sale.

And that was exactly what happened—boy, was this a great day, or what?—at Quark. Within ten minutes, the Quark management team was so mesmerized by the presentation and their own questions that they almost forgot Andy was there. Within ten minutes after that Andy knew they had the money, what they wanted and who would sign off on the deal. Forty-five minutes later, Andy was out of there with a $50 thousand signed contract for an initial order of 1000 units to be used in prototypes. If the product worked—and Quark survived—six months from now there'd be an order for 50,000 units more.

Andy set the phone to auto-answer, then turned on the radio and rolled down the windows. His destination was the monthly sales office meeting, and he grinned at the news he'd be able to tell the others. Top this, guys.

The monthly meeting was held in the banquet room of a local restaurant, the sales office itself having been reduced to a single rented room in an office building. It contained a tired old coffee maker, a credenza, three chairs, and a desk owned by the office manager, Greg Howell, who rarely showed up himself. Once each week, Howell tried to arrange a face-to-face with each of his people, but they were just as likely to meet in a restaurant or one of their homes.

It was only at the monthly meeting that the entire staff of the district sales office—all eleven salespeople plus Howell—got together, in Larry Stills' phrase, "to swap pheromones." Stills would be there; and the memory guy, Bob Lichte, who'd just helped him with Protectron (and did Andy have news for him—that new controller needed tons of memory). Mary Jean Hardy would be there too—"Mary Jean the Presentation Queen," who understood this technology even better than Andy, was the person the whole company sales force depended upon to tell Marketing just what they wanted in their presentations. Andy wanted to thank her for driving through that new Butterfly show-and-tell and to suggest to her a new presentation on the parallel-processing scheme.

It's funny, Andy thought, as he pulled off the turnpike. Back when we were all stuffed in that overgrown closet called a sales office, I used to get sick of seeing these people every day. Now I can't wait to be around them.

He pulled the car into a parking place in front of a bakery. One last stop, a final reminder from his software agent before Andy turned it off for the day. It was a cake decorated like a notebook computer. Andy had never forgotten Stills' words before that first visit to Protectron. Now Stills was the office's biggest computer enthusiast. That's why in a few minutes, in front of their assembled peers, Andy would present the computer/cake to Stills, saying, "Don't worry, Larry, it's not too big to eat."

VIRTUAL SELLING

Every element in Andy's story is possible right now. The only thing we lacked was a vision. Now we have it.

Recently history has shown that technology only succeeds when it begins and ends with the people who will use it. Virtual Selling succeeds where sales automation fails because, in the end, it is more *human*. And that essential humanity lies in the philosophy of Total Sales Quality.

This may seem like a contradiction. After all, how can messy humanity find a solution in a scheme that rests upon perfection?

The answer is that striving for perfection, even though we inevitably fall short, is what human beings do. It is what defines our lives and our work, it provides us with a way to measure our achievement.

The problem with the alternative, divergent model is not that it sets impossible goals, but that it has no goals at all. There is no absolute value by which to measure whether one is progressing or not. On the contrary, the only measure in this model is the one the system constructs for itself—and by that measure, success means only more and more technology, with no way to subtract the cost to morale, ambition, or self-respect. Thus, when The Conference Board surveyed sales automation systems in 1990, it found:

> Unexpected responses turned up as well, such as a lack of emphasis on "competitive advantage," apparent acceptance of "shadow" productivity gains instead of hard dollar advantages, and a pro forma approach to demonstrable dollar payback.[1]

As a result, these systems are expensive, onerous and, because there is no real goal, ultimately aimless. Unconstrained, they often produce results that are the antithesis of what they were designed to do: instead of supporting the sales force, they can enslave it; instead of bringing the customer into the process, they keep him or her at arm's length; instead of constructing a new and more efficient corporate hierarchy, they reinforce the old, unpractical one. But perhaps worst of all, because they measure success by their own terms, they create their own hermetic worlds in which there is no obvious way out except to buy more in an upward spiral of ever-greater investment and ever-deeper frustration.

The Informed Sales Force

If the fundamental task of the corporation is to sell, then the customer is the ultimate arbiter of the company's success. Given that, it follows that every action the company takes, and every decision it makes, must be in support of its relationship with that customer. Most of all, the individual sales rep, as the company's advocate in that relationship, must be at the very least the focal point of all of the company's energies. Technology helps not by stripping these salespeople of their power or stealing away time that could be spent with customers, but by increasing that time, and enhancing each contact. This is *Virtual Selling*.

But companies are vast and complicated structures, full of crosscurrents and sidepools of information and expertise. The only way to harness such an entity is to give it a common direction. And that is possible through a common, suitably distant and demanding, goal. The best such goal is a perfect correspondence between the needs of sales and the operations of the rest of the company. This is *Total Sales Quality.*

When an alignment occurs between the events at the customer/salesperson contact and the operation of the company itself, the salesperson is empowered with the total knowledge and talent of the organization. The company is now operating at its best. The salesperson repays the company's efforts by becoming its best and most knowledgeable representative. And when this is true of every member of the company's sales staff, the enterprise has reached its peak efficiency. This is an *Informed Sales Force*.

So there it is. When we properly begin with people and perfection, we create the same goal that Sales Force Automation has claimed all along. Only this time, we actually get there.

Notes

1. Finding the Path

1. *Personal Selling Power* (15th Anniversary Issue) (January 1995): 43.
2. Ken Dulaney, "Rethinking SFA," Sales Leadership Strategies conference presentation, Gartner Group, February 7, 1994.
3. M. Close, "Markets," Sales Leadership Strategies conference presentation, Gartner Group, February 7, 1994, p. 1.
4. MIRC USA, "New Developments in Sales Automation Software Markets" (MIRC USA, 1993): I-1.
5. Ibid.
6. Michael Sullivan-Trainor, "It's All in the Numbers," *Computerworld* (Sept. 13, 1993): 9.
7. Louis A. Wallis, "Changing Sales Roles with CSS," in Wallis, *Computer-Based Sales Force Support* (The Conference Board, Report No. 953, 1994): 11.
8. Ibid.
9. Rowland T. Moriarty and Gordon S. Swartz, "Automation to Boost Sales and Marketing," *Harvard Business Review* (January–February, 1989): 100.
10. Ibid.
11. Wallis, *Computer-Based Sales:* 7.
12. Ibid., 104.
13. *Electronic Business*, special advertising supplement prepared by Hewlett-Packard Co., October 1993.

14. Lewis Perelman, "Kanbrain," *Forbes ASAP* (June 6, 1994): 84.
15. Ibid.
16. Michael Adams, "Remote Control," *Performance* (March 1995): 46.
17. Thayer C. Taylor, "Going Mobile," *Sales & Marketing Management* (May 1994): 100.
18. Ibid.: 95.
19. Martin Everett, "It's No Fluke," *Sales & Marketing Management* (April 1994): 71.

2. Total Sales Quality

1. John W. Verity, "Taking a Laptop on a Call," *Business Week* (October 25, 1993): 124.
2. Andy Cohen, "Smooth Sailing," *Sales & Marketing Management* (March 1995): R10.
3. Mary Walton, *The Deming Management Method* (New York: Putnam [1988] c. 1986): 131–134.
4. Ibid.
5. Ibid.
6. Miller Heiman, *Strategic Selling* (New York: W. Morrow, 1985): 237.
7. Barry J. Trailer, "Measuring the Top Line: Sales Metric, Accountability, and More," speech delivered to DCI Field & Sales Force Automation Conference, Boston, June 8, 1995.

3. Making the Sale

1. Joseph Conlin, "Bazaar Behavior," *Sales & Marketing Management* (June 1995): 78–79.

4. The Hurried Pace of Change

1. Andy Cohen, "Going Mobile," *Sales & Marketing Management* special section, "The Road Warrior" (June 1994, Part 2): 5.
2. Ibid.
3. Ibid.
4. Case source: Martin Everett, "Vulcan Forges the Ties that Bind," *Sales & Marketing Management* (August 1992): 84–85.
5. Ibid.
6. Ibid.

7. Thayer C. Taylor, "Sales Automation Cuts the Cord," *Sales & Marketing Management* (1993): 110.

8. Ibid.

9. Case source: Melissa Campanelli, "Road Warrior/Wireless Communication," *Sales & Marketing Management* special section, "The Road Warrior" (June 1994, Part 2): 6.

10. Ibid.

11. Ibid.

12. Ibid.

13. Jeffrey Schwartz, "Newton Takes the Field," *Communications Week* (August 1, 1994): 70.

14. Ibid.

15. For more detailed information, consult Michael S. Malone, *The Microprocessor: A Biography* (New York: Telos/Springer-Verlag 1995).

16. Robert X. Cringely, "Who, What and Why of Wireless," *Forbes ASAP* (September 1993): 84 ff.

17. Tony Seideman, "Way Cool!," *Sales & Marketing Management* Part 2 (June 1994): 12.

18. Ginger Trumfio, "Don't Lose Time in the Trunk," *Sales & Marketing Management* (August 1994): 75.

5. Virtual Reality

1. "The material in this chapter is derived from Tom Siebel, "Technology Trends in Sales Automation," a speech delivered to the DCI Field & Sales Force Automation Conference held in December 1994 in Boston, and from William H. Davidow and Michael S. Malone, *The Virtual Corporation* (New York: HarperCollins), 1993.

6. Finding the Facts

1. Data from Doug Andrey, Semiconductor Industry Association (July 22, 1994).

2. Rowland Moriarty and Gordon Swartz, *Harvard Business Review* (January 1, 1989): 100–109.

3. Mike Fillon, "Keep on Trucking," *Sales & Marketing Management* (June 1995): 17.

4. Megan Santosus, "Pursuing the Perfect Pitch," *CIO* (June 1, 1994): 31.

5. Chuck Appleby, "A Dose of Strong Medicine," *Information Week* (February 7, 1994): 45.

6. Ibid.
7. Ibid.
8. Ibid.
9. Data from BusinessWire, Grid press release, January 4, 1991.
10. Ibid.
11. Ibid.
12. Ian Meiklejohn, "Window on the World," *Management Today* (U.K., July 1989): 113.
13. Ibid.

7. Total Quality Marketing

1. Stan Rapp and Tom Collins, *Maxi-Marketing* (New York: McGraw-Hill, 1988; softbound edition, New York: Plume Books, 1989).
2. Alvin Toffler, *The Third Wave* (New York: William Morrow & Co., 1980): 248.
3. See Davidow and Malone, *The Virtual Corporation.*
4. Edward Nash, "Prospecting for Leads," *Sales & Marketing Management* (February 1994), 33.
5. Rapp and Collins, *Maxi-Marketing* (softbound edition): 8.
6. The other two are Maximized Media (now encompassed by sales management and Virtual Selling) and Maximized Accountability, which is merely proving to management that the system works.
7. Ibid.: 32–33.
8. Allan J. Magrath, "Rethinking Your Strategy," *Sales & Marketing Management* (May 1994): 23.

8. Virtual Selling

1. Waters Chromatography is a much-covered case. This description is derived from *Forbes ASAP*, *Selling*, and *PCWeek*, as listed below.
2. George W. Colombo, "Presenting: A New Tool," *Selling* (June 1994): 29.
3. Mark Moore, "Staff Finds Freedom with Freelance," *PCWeek* (February 28, 1994): 29.
4. Ibid.
5. Alice LaPlante, "It's Wired Willy Loman," *Forbes ASAP* (April 11, 1994): 49.
6. Ibid: 30.
7. Tony Seideman, "On the Cutting Edge," *Sales & Marketing Management* (June 1994): 20.

8. Verity, "Taking a Laptop."
9. Ibid.
10. Thayer C. Taylor, "Show and Tell that Sell," *Sales & Marketing Management* (April 1990): 78.
11. Verity, "Taking a Laptop."
12. R. Lee Sullivan, "The Office that Never Closes," *Forbes* (May 23, 1994): 212.
13. LaPlante, "Willy Loman," 53.
14. Ibid.: 54
15. Jennifer deJong and Robert L. Scheler, "Virtual Selling," *Inc. Technology* (March 1995): 61.
16. Thayer C. Taylor, "It's Better to Show than Tell," *Sales & Marketing Management* (April 1994): 47.
17. Ibid.

9. Rethinking Sales Management

1. Michael Adams, "Remote Control," *Performance* (March 1995): 45.
2. Jerry Vass and Iris Herrin, "The VASS Company Study," *VASS Company* (April 1994).
3. Tony Seideman, "Who Needs Managers?" *Sales & Marketing Management* (August 1994): 16.
4. Stephen Gondert, "The 10 Biggest Mistakes of SFA (and How to Avoid Them)," *Sales & Marketing Management* (February 1993): 56.
5. Seideman, "Who Needs Managers?"
6. *Sales & Marketing Management*, "Restructuring Your Sales Force," *Sales & Marketing Management Manager's Handbook* (February 1994): 40.
7. Nancy Arnott, " 'Selling is Dying,' " *Sales & Marketing Management* (August 1994): 84.
9. Adams, "Remote Control," 47.
10. Ibid.

10. The Informed Sales Force

1. Wallis, *Computer-Based Sales*, 9.

Index

Index